MW00614176

The Comings of Christ

Why I Am a Partial Preterist

Harold R. Eberle

Worldcast Publishing
Yakima, Washington, USA

The Comings of Christ
Why I Am a Partial Preterist

© 2014 by Harold R. Eberle
First printing, July 2014

Worldcast Publishing
P.O. Box 10653
Yakima, WA 98909-1653
(509) 248-5837
www.worldcastpublishing.com
office@worldcastpublishing.com

ISBN 978-1-882523-41-2
Cover by Chris Ritchie
Final Editing, Amy Calkins

Unless otherwise stated, all biblical quotations are taken from the New American Standard Bible © 1977, The Lockman Foundation, La Habra, California 90631. Emphasis within Scripture quotations is the author's own.

ALL RIGHTS RESERVED

No part of this publication may be reproduced, stored in a retrieval system, or transmitted in any form or by any means—electronic, mechanical, photocopy, recording, or otherwise—without the express prior permission of Worldcast Publishing Company, with the exception of brief excerpts in magazine articles and/or reviews.

Requests for translating into other languages should be addressed to Worldcast Publishing.

Printed in the United States of America

Table of Contents

Introduction 1

1. What Prophecies Fulfilled? 5
2. Questions of Matthew 24:3 9
3. What Is His Coming? 13
4. End of the Age of Judaism? 19
5. End of What Age? 23
6. Coming Day of Judgment 29
7. His Second Coming? 35
8. All Things Fulfilled? 43
9. Revelation Events Are Near 47
10. Reading the Revelation 51
11. Second Set of Judgments 57
12. Covenant or Kingdom? 65
13. The Return and Marriage 71
14. The Millennial Reign 75
15. Satan Thrown into the Abyss? 79
16. The Great White Throne? 83
17. Resurrection of the Dead 85
18. New Heaven and Earth 93
19. Redemption of Creation 99
20. Anti-Semitism?..103

In Closing 109
Other Books by Harold R. Eberle 115

Introduction

Among Christians who are already involved in discussions about preterism, these topics raise heated debates. However, most Christians today have little understanding of what preterism is all about, so let me explain the fundamentals. A simple overview will guarantee that we are all starting on the same page.

Eschatology refers to the study of end-times. Various Christian groups have different eschatological views even though they all attempt to develop their views from the Bible. We can categorize the various views in different ways. One way is to refer to these three theological labels:

1. **Futurism**
2. **Full Preterism**
3. **Partial Preterism**

Each of these labels corresponds to the time period during which end-time prophecies in the Bible are fulfilled. To simplify explanations, teachers usually refer to the end-time prophecies recorded in Matthew 24 and the Book of Revelation.

The view that says those prophecies will be fulfilled in the future is called *futurism*. The view that claims those prophecies have already been fulfilled is called *full preterism* (from the Latin *praeteritus*, meaning "gone by" or "past"). *Partial preterism* is a mediating view between futurism and full preterism, because it sees some of the end-time prophecies fulfilled in the future and some in the past.

Eschatological View	Matthew 24 & Revelation
1. Futurism:	all fulfilled in the future
2. Full Preterism:	all fulfilled in the past
3. Partial Preterism:	part future, part past

In modern Evangelical churches, the most commonly taught view is the futurist view; however, this book is not written for those who hold the futurist view. I coauthored another book with Pastor Martin Trench in which we address the issues of futurism and explain how many of the eschatological prophecies were fulfilled in A.D. 70 when Jerusalem was destroyed. If you believe there will be a future Antichrist and Great Tribulation, then you are a futurist. This book may not even make sense to you, so you will be much better off if you first read our book entitled *Victorious Eschatology*.[1]

The focus of this book is on distinguishing the partial preterist view from the full preterist view and then explaining why I believe partial preterism is the view that corresponds most closely with the Bible.

Before we jump into the relevant issues, it is important that we get our terminology correct. In this book, I will be using the labels, *partial preterism* and *full preterism*. However, you should know that when you read the writings of other Christians (*e.g.*, those who are posting articles on the internet), you may find several different labels being used to refer to partial preterism and full preterism.

For example, adherents of both views like to claim the shortened label *preterism* for their own view. By this, I mean that there are some adherents of partial preterism who call their own view *preterism* while labeling their opponents' view as *full preterism*. At the same time there are some adherents of full preterism who label their own view *preterism* while labeling their opponent's view *partial preterism*.

Adherents of each view also like to use labels that put their own view in a positive light. Of course, this is only natural, and

---

1 Information on how to obtain *Victorious Eschatology* can be found in the back of this book.

we can see similar dynamics in many discussions between opposing views. For example, in the current debate concerning abortion, people do not like to be labeled pro-abortion or anti-abortion. Rather than pro-abortion, adherents would rather be labeled pro-choice. Rather than anti-abortion, adherents would rather be labeled pro-life. Not only do these labels put their position in a more positive light, but adherents of each view would say the positive labels express their own view more accurately.

Similar struggles over terminology happen in discussions about eschatology. Both partial and full preterists have more positive labels by which they like to be known. The most used labels are listed below.

Other Labels Used for Two Eschatological Views

Partial Preterism	**Full Preterism**
Orthodox Preterism	Consistent Preterism
Classical Preterism	Consistent Eschatology
Moderate Preterism	Fulfilled Eschatology
Partial Futurism	Covenant Eschatology

Some of these labels serve a two-fold purpose—putting one's own view in a positive light while putting the opposing view in a negative light. For example, when partial preterists call their own view *orthodox preterism*, they are implying that full preterism is unorthodox. When full preterists call their own view *consistent preterism*, they are implying that partial preterism is inconsistent.

In addition to these labels, there are some that are purposely degrading of the opposing view. For example, partial preterists sometimes label full preterism as *hyper-preterism*.

Although you should be aware of these labels when you read other writings on this subject, I will keep things simple in this book—and refrain from using emotion-stirring labels—by only using the labels *partial preterism* and *full preterism*.

Before jumping into this, I want to honor my brothers and sisters who hold to the full preterist view. I know it is with sincerity of heart that they take the stand that they do. They desire to bring truth to the Church, and they are committed to the inspiration of the Bible.

However, they have set in concrete a certain understanding of the *parousia*[2] with which partial preterists like myself disagree. In particular, they have decided the parousia is the Second Coming of Jesus, and that Second Coming happened in A.D. 70. Once they have fixed this date in their own minds, the rest of their conclusions logically follow.

So then, I am not challenging their sincerity, their love of the Church, their commitment to the Bible, or their logical integrity. I reject their system of thought, which is based on a misunderstanding of the parousia.[3]

---

2 & 3 *Parousia* is a Greek word that means, "coming" or "arrival."

Chapter 1
What Prophecies Fulfilled?

Partial and full preterists agree that many end-time prophecies were fulfilled in A.D. 70. That was the year Jerusalem was destroyed. A Roman general named Titus led 20,000 soldiers to surround Jerusalem and cut off all supplies of food so the people would starve. After several months the soldiers came into the city and mercilessly killed more than one million Jews. When the soldiers entered the Temple, they slit the throats of more than 2,000 Jews and then set the building on fire.

Partial and Full Preterists Agree

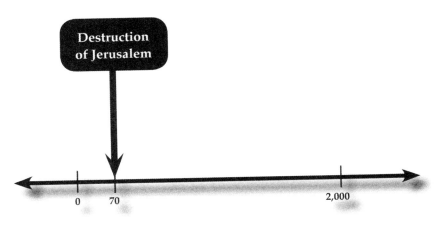

The destruction of Jerusalem and the Temple marked the end of the Jewish religious system. God no longer wanted anyone to approach Him through priests or the sacrificing of animals. We have a new High Priest who has made the ultimate and final sacrifice. Partial and full preterists agree about these truths.

However, they disagree about the timing of most other eschatological events. Among those events are the following:

- The Second Coming of Jesus
- The Marriage of Jesus and His Bride
- The Millennium
- The Resurrection of the Dead
- The Great White Throne Judgment
- Creation of the New Heaven and Earth

Full preterists teach that all of the events listed above took place by A.D. 70 when Jerusalem was destroyed.

Full Preterist View

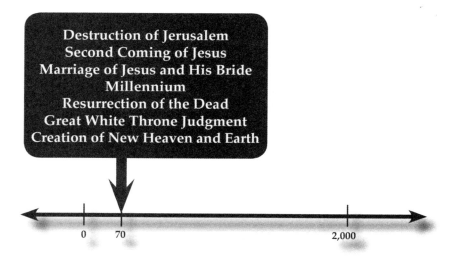

In contrast, partial preterists teach that all or many of the events listed above will happen in the future. They still see A.D. 70 as a significant event in fulfilling many things that were prophesied in the Bible. However, partial preterists believe the Second Coming of Jesus, the marriage of Jesus and His Bride, the resurrection of the dead, and the Great White Throne Judgment will happen in the future.

The Partial Preterist View

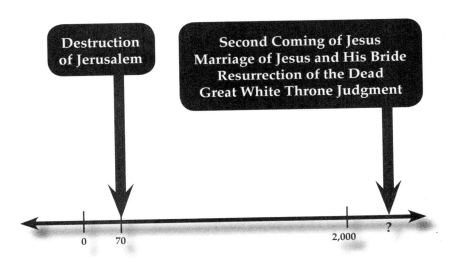

In the diagram above I did not insert the Millennium or the creation of the new Heaven and Earth, because not all partial preterists agree about when these two events are fulfilled.

Because of these differences, teachers of eschatology often make finer distinctions between two types of partial preterism: *historical preterism* and *modern preterism*.

Two Forms of Partial Preterism
Historical Preterism
Modern Preterism

Historical preterism (which I hold) says the events described in the Book of Revelation are fulfilled over the course of history. Most adherents of historical preterism say Revelation 1 to 11 was fulfilled by A.D. 70, while Revelation 12 to 22 happen(ed) after A.D. 70.[4] This distinction will become evident later when we provide an overview of the Book of Revelation. Among those holding to historical preterism are such noted teachers as John Calvin, Martin Luther, and Charles Spurgeon.

The other form of partial preterism—*modern preterism*—has been of more recent development. Adherents teach that the events of Revelation 1 to 18 happened by A.D. 70, but some of the events in Revelation 19 to 22 will happen in the future. Among those holding to modern preterism are such noted teachers/authors as N. T. Wright, David Chilton, and Gary De-Mar.

For most readers, the distinction between historical preterism and modern preterism will not have significant meaning, but for those who are serious students of eschatology, this is worth noting. I hold to historical preterism. Therefore, in the following pages I will be contrasting partial preterism with full preterism, but readers who are astute students of eschatology will want to keep in mind that the type of partial preterism to which I adhere is historical preterism.

Partial Preterism————Versus————Full Preterism
(Historical Preterism)

---

4 Some teachers use the label "mild preterist."

Chapter 2
Questions of Matthew 24:3

The major differences between partial and full preterism become evident when we study Matthew 24. There we see Jesus talking to His disciples in what has become known as the Olivet Discourse. In Matthew 24:3, the disciples asked Jesus:

> *Tell us, when will these things happen, and what will be the sign of Your coming, and of the end of the age?*

Jesus answered these questions in the rest of Matthew 24 and 25. How we understand His answer is determined by how we understand the questions the disciples asked.

Partial and full preterists agree that the first question, *"When will these things happen?"*, is about the destruction of Jerusalem that happened in A.D. 70. This follows logically when a person reads Matthew 23, where Jesus rebuked the Jewish religious leaders and prophesied that Jerusalem and the Temple would be destroyed (Matt. 23:35-38). Realizing that there is no break between Matthew 23 and 24, we see how Jesus and the disciples came out of the Temple and immediately went up on the Mount of Olives, where they were looking directly at the Temple.[5] The first question on the disciples' minds was, "When will Jerusalem and the Temple be destroyed?"

---

5 The parallel passage in Mark 13:1-3 makes this clear.

In two passages, Jesus said that the destruction would happen within that generation:

> *Truly I say to you, all these things will come upon this generation.*
>
> (Matt. 23:36)

> *Truly I say to you, this generation will not pass away until all these things take place.*
>
> (Matt. 24:34)

Both partial and full preterists take these words of Jesus literally. Jesus said these words around A.D. 30, and therefore, the prophecies that Jesus made about the destruction of Jerusalem had to have been fulfilled by A.D. 70.[6] Indeed, Jerusalem was destroyed exactly as Jesus prophesied.

In Matthew 24, Jesus gave several signs that the disciples could watch for that would precede the destruction of Jerusalem. He told of:

- people claiming to be Christ (vs. 5)
- wars and rumors of war (vs. 6)
- famines and earthquakes (vs. 7)
- persecution (vs. 9)
- a falling away (vs. 10)
- false prophets arising (vs. 11)
- gospel of the Kingdom preached to the world (vs. 15)

Partial and full preterists agree that all of these signs happened in the generation of those people who were actually listening to Jesus' words at that time. All of these signs happened before the destruction of Jerusalem, exactly as Jesus said.

Christians who have only been taught futurism will have a difficult time understanding how these signs were all fulfilled by A.D. 70, since they have been taught that these signs will all

---

6 In the Bible, a generation was considered 40 years in length, as can be seen when the Hebrew people wandered in the wilderness for 40 years until a generation passed away.

happen in our future. As we stated earlier, this book is not written to answer the questions of futurists, and for this reason I ask that Christians who have been taught the futurists view to read *Victorious Eschatology* before reading this book.

Still, it is worth quickly explaining the one sign that futurists have the most difficulty understanding as fulfilled by A.D. 70—that the gospel of the Kingdom was preached to the whole world (Matt. 24:15). Several Bible passages tell us the gospel was preached in the whole world during the lifetime of Jesus' disciples:

> But I say, surely they have never heard, have they? Indeed they have; "Their voice has gone out into all the earth, And their words to the ends of the world."
>
> (Rom. 10:18)

> Now to Him who is able to establish you according to my gospel...has been made known to all the nations,
>
> (Rom. 16:25-26)

> ...the gospel that you have heard, which was proclaimed in all creation under heaven, and of which I, Paul, was made a minister.
>
> (Col. 1:23)

Paul made it clear that the gospel was preached in the whole world during his lifetime (see also Rom. 1:8 and Col. 1:5-6).[7]

We could take time to explain how the other signs were fulfilled by A.D. 70, but that would steer us away from our primary goal of comparing partial and full preterism. Both partial and full preterists agree that all of the signs Jesus spoke of in Matthew 24:4-15 happened by A.D. 70.

---

7 It is helpful to know that the Greek word that has been translated as *world* in Matthew 24:15, is *oikoumene*, which literally refers to the *civilized world*. During the first century, this word was typically used to refer to the Roman Empire, so Jesus was saying that the gospel would be preached to the whole Roman Empire before Jerusalem was destroyed.

Partial and full preterists also agree that Matthew 24:16-28 is describing the actual destruction of Jerusalem in A.D. 70. Jesus warned people to flee from Judea because a great tribulation would take place in that region. Jesus ended that passage by referring to the corpse where the vultures will gather. This is descriptive of the city of Jerusalem, which laid as a corpse after her destruction. The vultures were symbolic of the Roman army because at that time in history the vulture was the insignia under which the Roman soldiers went to war.

Partial and full preterists agree that Matthew 24:4-28 records Jesus' answer to the first question that the disciples asked: "When will these things happen?"

Where partial and full preterists disagree is in how to understand the rest of Matthew 24 and 25. To see their disagreement, consider again the questions the disciples asked Jesus:

> *Tell us, when will these things happen, and what will be the sign of Your coming, and of the end of the age?*

Partial preterists point out that there are three distinct questions here:

1) When will these things happen?
2) What will be the sign of Your coming?
3) [When will be] the end of the age?

Seeing three different questions, partial preterists expect Jesus to offer a different answer for each question.

In contrast, full preterists say the disciples were only asking one question, but stating it in three different ways. Full preterists believe the disciples were only asking about the events that happened by A.D. 70. Therefore, full preterists understand the answer Jesus gave in all of Matthew 24 and 25 as fulfilled by A.D. 70.

This identifies a clear distinction between partial and full preterists. In coming pages we will explain why this distinction is important and what the implications are.

Chapter 3
What Is His Coming?

Partial and full preterists agree that when the disciples asked, *"When will these things happen?"* they were asking about when the destruction of Jerusalem would take place. However, they disagree about the second question, *"What will be the sign of Your coming?"* (Matt. 24:3).

Please note that this question is not about the *first* coming of Jesus. Everyone agrees that the first coming of Jesus took place when He was born in Bethlehem. Here we are discussing how the phrase is used to talk about another coming of the Lord. In particular, what were the disciples of Jesus thinking when they asked Jesus, *"What will be the sign of Your coming?"*

Full preterists understand "the coming" to be when Jesus came to judge Jerusalem in A.D. 70.

Partial preterists, such as myself, say that "the coming" asked about in Matthew 24:3 does not refer to that event. We can affirm this partial preterist view by looking at two different time references that Jesus made. In Matthew 10:23, Jesus said:

> But whenever they persecute you in one city, flee to the next; for truly I say to you, you will not finish going through the cities of Israel until the <u>Son of Man comes</u>.

Jesus refers to when *"the Son of Man comes."* Jesus told His disciples this event would take place before they finished *"going through the cities of Israel."*

However, Jesus gave us a different time reference in Matthew 24:15:

> *This gospel of the kingdom shall be preached in the whole world as a testimony to all the nations, and then the end will come.*

Both partial and full preterists agree this verse was fulfilled right before the destruction of A.D. 70.

Certainly the disciples finished *"going through the cities of Israel"* before they finished preaching *"in the whole world."* Yet, Jesus said the date when *"the Son of Man comes"* would be *before* they finished going through Israel. The judgment of Jerusalem would be *after* they finished preaching to the whole world. This reveals two distinct events.

The Coming of the Son:

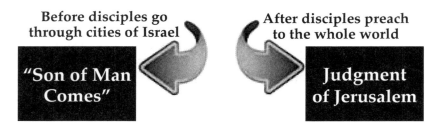

Full preterists ignore this distinction. They equate the Son of Man coming with the judgment of Jerusalem. This is in spite of the fact that the time references given above prove that these events took place at different times.

Once we have determined that the date when *"the Son of Man comes"* is not equivalent to the destruction of Jerusalem, we can go back to study the disciples' questions. To understand what those disciples were asking we must put ourselves in their shoes 2,000 years ago. What were they thinking when they asked Jesus, *"What will be the sign of your coming?"*

The Jewish people of that time period were looking for God to send a Messiah. They wanted a King. That was their great hope. The prophets had foretold it many times. The Jews were looking for the Man who would sit on the throne of David (1 Chron. 17:11-14). They were looking for the One who would crush Satan's head. The Jews of the first century were looking to God to send a Redeemer who would set them free of oppression. They believed a Kingdom would be established and it would endure forever (Dan. 2:44; 7:13-14; Is. 9:6-7).

They were *not* looking for someone to come and destroy Jerusalem. They wanted a King—not to destroy them but to lead them to victory!

This corresponds to the message Jesus and the disciples had been preaching throughout Judea. They had been declaring, "The Kingdom of God is at hand!" This was on the forefront of their thoughts. So they wanted to know when Jesus would come into the Kingdom that they had been preaching about for the previous three years.

This understanding of "the coming" was so common among the Jewish people of the first century that even the thief who died on the cross next to Jesus said:

> *Jesus, remember me when* **You come in Your kingdom!**
> (Luke 23:42)

The thief was not saying, "Jesus, remember me when you come to destroy Jerusalem." That would have made no sense. The thief was about to die. He was not even going to be alive on Earth when Jerusalem was destroyed. The thief was asking Jesus to remember him when He became enthroned as King!

We can see this was on the minds of James and John when they said to Jesus, *"Grant that we may sit, one on Your right and one on Your left, in Your glory"* (Mark 10:37). They were not asking if they could sit on Jesus' right and left hand while He destroyed Jerusalem. They were asking if they could sit at Jesus' right and left hand when Jesus came into His Kingdom.

Daniel had seen a vision of the Messiah coming into His Kingdom:

One like a Son of Man was coming,
And He came up to the Ancient of Days
And was presented before Him.
And to Him was given dominion,
Glory and a kingdom,

(Dan. 7:13-14)

Every person trained in Jewish tradition knew these words. On the forefront of their thoughts was the Son of Man coming before God to receive authority and a Kingdom.

When did that happen? After Jesus died, rose from the dead, and ascended into Heaven: *"He was received up into heaven and sat down at the right hand of God"* (Mark 16:19). All authority was given to Jesus, both in Heaven and on Earth. Jesus came into His Kingdom the moment He ascended into Heaven and sat down next to the Father. It happened in A.D. 30.[8]

This understanding is contrary to the full preterist view, which equates the coming of Jesus to the destruction of Jerusalem. Of course, both of these events happened within the first generation, but Jesus used different terminology when He referred to these two events:

...you will not finish going through the cities of Israel until the **Son of Man comes**.

(Matt. 10:23)

...there are some of those who are standing here who will not taste death until they see the **kingdom of God after it has come with power.**

(Mark 9:1)

One event is referred to as the *Son of Man comes*. The second event is referred to as the *Kingdom of God comes with power*. The first happened before the disciples finished going through the cities of Israel (A.D. 30). The second happened after they finished preaching the gospel of the Kingdom throughout the

---

8 Some historians argue about the year of Jesus's ascension, but I will use A.D. 30 since the exact year of Jesus' ascension is not critical for this discussion.

world (A.D. 70).

Jesus' Coming Versus the Kingdom Coming with Power

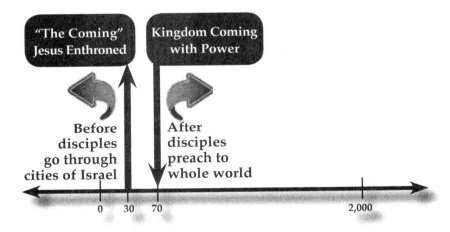

A Bible passage that will lock in this understanding is in Luke 19, where Jesus compared Himself to a nobleman who had to go to a distant country to receive a kingdom:

> *So He said, "A nobleman went to a distant country to receive a kingdom for himself, and then return..."*
> (Luke 19:11-12)

Indeed, Jesus died, resurrected, and ascended into Heaven. When He ascended, all authority was given to Him over Heaven and Earth. He was enthroned. He came into His Kingdom.

Jesus went on in the same parable to explain that after the nobleman received his kingdom, he returned to judge his servants and his enemies. Concerning his enemies, the nobleman said:

> *But these enemies of mine, who did not want me to reign over them, bring them here and slay them in my presence.*
> (Luke 19:27)

In like fashion, Jesus ascended into Heaven in A.D. 30, and then He returned in A.D. 70 to judge His enemies who lived in Jerusalem.

This clarification alone completely undermines full preterism. Their entire system of thought is built on equating the coming of Jesus to the destruction of Jerusalem in A.D. 70. This will become more evident as we continue.

Chapter 4
End of the Age of Judaism?

In the last chapter, we identified "the coming" mentioned in Matthew 24:3 as the enthronement of Jesus as King. Once this truth is established, we can look at Matthew 24:3 through different eyes. The disciples asked Jesus:

> *Tell us, when will these things happen, and what will be the sign of Your coming, and of the end of the age?*

As we explained, full preterists see this verse as one question, stated in three different ways. In reality, there are three questions: The first question is about the destruction of Jerusalem, and the second question is about the Lord's coming into His Kingdom. Seeing this distinction disrupts the full preterist's fixation that all three questions are one. Now that we see the disciples' questions as distinct, we must discover what the third question is. What were the disciples thinking when they asked Jesus about "the end of the age"?

The KJV words this phrase as, "the end of the world" Both partial and full preterists agree that the insertion of the word *world* reveals the bias of the translators of the KJV. The Greek word here is *aion*, which definitely means "age."

So what did the disciples mean by "the end of the age"?

Full preterists need this question to be about events that happened at the time of the destruction of Jerusalem. Therefore, they need to find some age that ended in A.D. 70. What full preterists have decided is that A.D. 70 was the end of the Jewish age.

But that cannot be true. When the disciples were sitting with Jesus on the Mount of Olives 2,000 years ago, they could not have been thinking about the end of the age of Judaism.

To see this, we must put ourselves back in their shoes. It is easy for us to look back and evaluate the events of A.D. 70 from our perspective today. We can see that, indeed, dramatic events took place when Jerusalem was destroyed, but Jesus' disciples did not have our perspective. At that time in history, they were still trying to understand some of the truths that today Christians consider basic. Several times Jesus tried to explain to His disciples that He was going to suffer and die, but they could not seem to even grasp this (*e.g.,* Matt. 16:21-23). Before Jesus died, the disciples did not understand how our Lord's death would take care of our sins, let alone bring an end to the age of Judaism. That is not what they were thinking when they were sitting with Jesus on the Mount of Olives.

Furthermore, the disciples believed Jesus was the *Jewish* Messiah. He was going to sit on the throne of David and establish a Kingdom. Like every good Jew of that period, the disciples believed God was sending a Messiah to set their own people free of oppression. They did not think the Jewish age was ending. Quite to the contrary, they were looking for the fulfillment of God's promises to the Jews. They were looking for their finest hour when the Jewish Messiah would lead their nation to victory. This is evident in the disciples' question as recorded in Acts 1:6:

> *Lord, is it at this time You are restoring the kingdom to Israel?*

The disciples asked this question after Jesus had risen from the dead. Even at that time, the disciples still thought Jesus was going to raise up Israel to be the head of His Kingdom.

The disciples thought of Jesus' ministry as Jewish for many

years. Peter did not get the revelation that Gentiles could be a member of God's covenant people until Acts 10 when he met Cornelius. After that revelation, Peter and Paul had to work hard to convince the other early Church leaders that God had extended grace to the Gentiles. It was not until Acts 15 (around 20 years later) that the apostles settled the issue as to whether or not Gentiles had to keep the Jewish Laws.

Therefore, in Matthew 24:3, when the disciples asked Jesus about the end of the age, they could not have been asking about the end of the age of Judaism. That was not even in their frame of reference.

Chapter 5
End of What Age?

What were the disciples thinking when they asked Jesus about *"the end of the age"* (Matt. 24:3)?

To answer this, we first need to note that there are many different ages mentioned in the Bible. For example, Ecclesiastes 1:10 talks about the *"ages which were before us."* Romans 16:25 talks about *"long ages past."* First Corinthians 2:7 refers to that which *"God predestined before the ages."* Titus 1:2 talks about *"long ages ago."* Not only does the Bible talk about ages in the past, but Paul wrote of his current age referring to it as *"this present evil age"* (Gal. 1:4). Other passages talk about ages in the future; for example, Ephesians 2:7 refers to *"the ages to come."* Then in Hebrews 6:2 we read about *"the powers of the age to come"* (Heb. 6:5). Paul wrote, *"Not only in this age but also in the one to come"* (Eph. 1:21). Paul even talks about Jesus who is *"the King of ages"* (1 Tim. 1:17).[9] Ages come and ages go, but Jesus is King of all ages.

The point is that the word *age* (*aion*) did not refer to any one period of time in the Bible. It was a general term just like it is in the English language. *Age* can be used to refer to any long time period.

So what long time period were the disciples asking Jesus about?

To answer this, we must see things from their perspective 2,000 years ago. What was relevant to them? To understand

---

9 This is translated directly from the Greek.

Jewish thinking of that time period, we must separate ourselves from modern explanations of end-times, which are numerous and varied. We must go back to study the Jewish teachings of the first century.

The Jews living in the time of Jesus commonly believed:

1) A Messiah, born of the family of David, will come and establish a Kingdom;

2) The Messiah's Kingdom will battle and overcome all of the enemies of the Jews.

3) The Messiah's Kingdom will triumph, ushering in an age of worldwide peace and prosperity—known as the Messianic Age.

This was the most common understanding of Jews living in the first century. They were looking for the Messiah to come, establish a Kingdom, and bring in the Messianic Age.[10]

Most Common Jewish Eschatology in the First Century

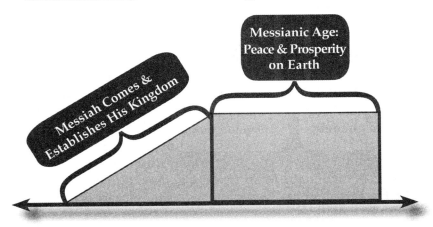

---

10 Three of the many places that offer this understanding are:
    B. *Talmud* Sanhedrin 98a;
    Talmud Sanhedrin 97a;
    Maimonides, *Commentary on Mishnah*, Sanhedrin 10:1.

The Jews believed the Messianic Age would be the period when Isaiah 2:4 would be fulfilled:

And He [Messiah] will judge between the nations,
And will render decisions for many peoples;
And they will hammer their swords into plowshares and
their spears into pruning hooks.
Nation will not lift up sword against nation,
And never again will they learn war.

Not only would there be worldwide peace, but the Messianic Age would also be the time when *"the wolf will dwell with the Lamb,"* *"the nursing child will play by the hole of the cobra,"* and *"the earth will be full of the knowledge of the Lord"* (Is. 11:6-9).

Of course, we do not need to accept the Jewish worldview; however, we would be foolish to ignore it. This was the most commonly understood eschatological view of the Jews while Jesus walked this earth. When Jesus talked to the people of His day, He was communicating to them so they could understand. He was working within their frame of reference. Therefore, we should consider their point of view when we try to understand Jesus' words to them.

The Jews developed their understanding from promises God had given them. Daniel explained that the Kingdom would be like a rock that would come into the Earth, then grow into a mountain, and then continue growing until it filled the Earth (Dan. 2:36-45). Isaiah explained that God would send a Child and grant that Child all authority; Isaiah wrote that there would be *"no end to the increase of His government or of peace"* (Is. 9:6-7).

Jesus expounded more about this Kingdom growth, telling the people that the Kingdom would grow like seeds in soil or yeast in dough (Matt. 13). Jesus explained to His disciples that the Kingdom would start as the smallest of all seeds but grow to be the biggest plant in the garden (Matt. 13:31-32).

As Jews listening to Jesus, the disciples would have formed an image in their minds of the Messiah setting up God's Kingdom, then that Kingdom growing until the Messianic Age came.

Jesus' Teaching about the Kingdom of God

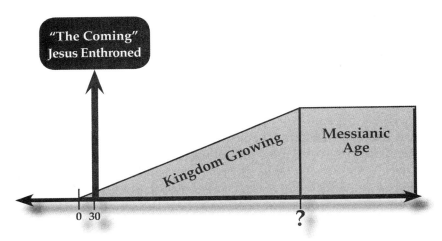

The disciples believed Jesus was the Messiah and the Kingdom of God was at hand. They had heard Jesus preach about it for three years. The disciples were excited to be living at the time in history when the Messiah had arrived and His Kingdom was being established.

Knowing the Messiah had arrived, they also wanted to know how long it would take for His Kingdom to establish peace and prosperity throughout the world. They understood the Messianic Age would be the total triumph of God's Kingdom here on Earth. Like all good Jews, they envisioned a day when the Messiah would reign on Earth, resulting in peace and prosperity for all of humanity.

So now we can go back to Matthew 24:3, where the disciples asked Jesus about the *"end of the age."* What were they asking? They believed they were in the age during which Messiah had come and He was establishing His Kingdom. So they were asking when that age would end and, hence, usher in the Messianic Age of perfect peace and prosperity.

The End of the Age in the Minds of Jesus' Disciples

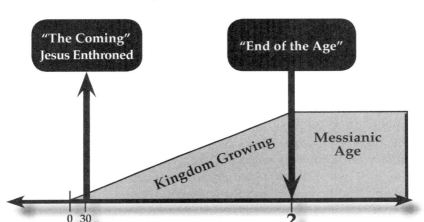

Let me re-emphasize that the disciples understood that they were already living in the age of the growing Kingdom. For three years, they had been following Jesus and listening to Him declare that the Kingdom of God was at hand. They heard Jesus explain that He was the Sower who was sowing good seeds in the soil (Matt. 13:37). Jesus made it clear that those seeds were the seeds of the Kingdom growing in the Earth (Matt. 13:19, 24, 38). The disciples themselves had been out preaching that the Kingdom of God was at hand. By healing the sick, they had been demonstrating to the people that the they were in the age of the growing Kingdom.

Of course, the Bible talks about other ages. As we explained, the word *age* (*aion*) simply referred to a long time period. But here we are determining *which* age the disciples were asking about when they sat on the Mount of Olives 2,000 years ago. We explained how they could not have been asking about the end of the age of Judaism, because at that time, they had no thoughts of Judaism ending. They had to be asking about the age in which they believed they were in—the age of the growing Kingdom.

To confirm this understanding, notice how Jesus used the phrase, *"end of the age"* when He gave the Great Commission:

> *All authority has been given to Me in heaven and on earth. Go therefore and make disciples of all the nations... teaching them to observe all that I commanded you; and lo, I am with you always, even to the **end of the age.***
>
> (Matt. 28:18-20)

The "age" Jesus referred to was during the time when the disciples were commissioned to *"make disciples of all nations."* Therefore, the *"end of that age"* would be the transition point between the growing Kingdom and the Messianic Age.

Chapter 6
Coming Day of Judgment

In the previous chapter, we explained the Jewish eschatological expectations during the first century and saw how Jews commonly believed God would send a Messiah to usher in a Messianic Age of worldwide peace and prosperity. If we consider Matthew 24:3 through that Jewish worldview, it is natural to conclude that Jesus' disciples were asking about the end of the age in which they were living—the age during which the Kingdom was being established on Earth.

The best way to confirm this understanding is to examine the answer Jesus gave to the disciples' question in Matthew 24:3. If His answer corresponds with the question, then we have good reason to believe we have understood the disciples' question correctly.

Here is how we can identify Jesus' answer. Remember that the disciples asked three questions in Matthew 24:3, and then Jesus answered those questions in the rest of Matthew 24 and all of chapter 25. This is one long discourse. Mark 13 and Luke 21 record the same discourse with one important difference. Matthew records three questions, while Mark and Luke only recorded the questions about the destruction of Jerusalem. For some reason that we do not know, Mark and Luke left off the third question about the end of the age.

The Disciples' Questions		
Matthew 24:3	Mark 13:4	Luke 21:7
Tell us, when will these things happen, and what will be the sign of Your coming, and of **the end of the age**?	*Tell us, when will these things be, and what will be the sign when all these things are going to be fulfilled?*	*Teacher, when therefore will these things happen? And what will be the sign when these things are about to take place?*

This gives us a helpful guide in understanding the answers Jesus gave to His disciples. This is true because Matthew goes on for much longer than Mark and Luke. Where Mark and Luke end, but Matthew goes on, we can expect the answer for the third question.

Jesus' Answer to the First Questions		
Matt. 24:4-25:46	Mark 13:5-37	Luke 21:8-36
false Christs	false Christs	false Christs
wars	wars	wars
earthquakes	earthquakes	earthquakes
famines	famines	famines
persecutions	persecutions	persecutions
false prophets		signs
falling away		
betrayals	betrayals	betrayals
gospel preached	gospel preached	
Abomination	Abomination	Jerusalem surrounded
flee Judea	flee Judea	flee Judea
tribulation	tribulation	days of vengeance
false Christs		
corpse & vultures		
signs in sun and moon	signs in sun and moon	signs in sun and moon
Son of Man coming	Son of Man coming	Son of Man coming
angels gathering elect	angels gathering elect	
fig tree	fig tree	fig tree
this generation	this generation	this generation
keep alert	keep alert	keep alert

Jesus' Answer to the Third Question		
Matt. 24:4-25:46	Mark 13:5-37	Luke 21:8-36
parable of ten virgins parable of talents Son of Man coming in glory to judge nations		

What do we find in Matthew's account that is not in Mark's or Luke's? Matthew goes on with:

1. Jesus' parable of the ten virgins (Matt. 25:1-13)
2. His parable of the talents (Matt. 25: 14-30)
3. His explanation of His future coming in glory with all His angels to judge the world (Matt. 25:31-46)

Each of these three accounts talks about a coming judgment—a day when people will be held accountable for their actions.

Consider Jesus' explanation of His coming in glory with all the angels:

> But when the **Son of Man comes in His glory, and all the angels with Him**, then He will sit on His glorious throne. All the nations will be gathered before Him; and He will separate them from one another, as the shepherd separates the sheep from the goats....
>
> (Matt. 25:31-33)

Jesus went on to explain how the King will welcome into His Kingdom those who fed Him, gave drink to Him, visited Him, and clothed Him by taking care of any of His brothers. So then, we see that the end of the age is associated with a day of judgment.

Notice that this passage talks about *"all the nations"* being gathered before Jesus. This is not just a judgment of a small group of people living in Jerusalem or Judea. Unlike the earlier part of the discourse in Matthew 24, Jesus is *not* talking about people fleeing from Judea. Jesus is talking about judgment of the whole world—a judgment that has not yet happened and, therefore, must happen in the future.

Also, take note of the terminology used to describe this worldwide day of judgment—***Son of Man comes in His glory, and all the angels with Him.*** This is different than ***the Son of Man coming*** and it is different than ***the Kingdom coming in power***. These are three different events identified as occurring at different times.

The Son of Man Coming in Glory with All of His Angels

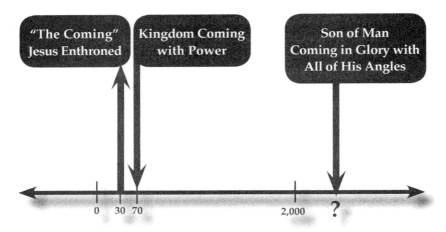

This fits perfectly with the worldview held by the first century Jews and the disciples of Jesus. Our Lord explained that at the end of the age He would come in glory with all of His angels. Then all of the nations would stand before Him for judgment. Then those who are considered sheep would be welcomed into His Kingdom—that is, they would be welcomed into the Messianic Age of perfect peace and prosperity. As we identified earlier, the end of the age is the transition point between the growing Kingdom and the Messianic Age.

The End of the Age Will Be a Day of Judgment

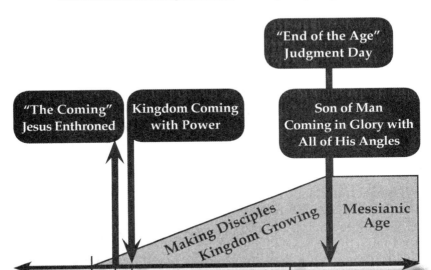

Of course, full preterists disagree. They interpret Matthew 24 and 25 through their lens of seeing all things fulfilled by A.D. 70. They see the coming, the Kingdom coming in power, and the Son of Man coming in glory with all of His angels as the same event. They even equate the judgment of Jerusalem with the judgment when *"all the nations will be gathered before Him"* (Matt. 25:32).

Full preterists sometimes refer to the phrase *"all the nations will be gathered"* as a "difficult" phrase, but the only reason it is difficult for them is because it does not fit into their preconceived time frame. The judgment of Jerusalem is not the same as the judgment of all the nations.

In contrast, the partial preterist explanation comes from a straightforward reading of the text. Jesus will come in His glory and all the angels with Him to judge all the nations. It is simple if we just accept it as fact.

The judgment of all the nations will happened at the end of

the age. The end of which age? The age we are presently in. The same age the early disciples were in. The age during which the Kingdom is growing in the Earth and Jesus' followers are making disciples of all the nations.

This understanding also fits perfectly with the parables of the talents and ten virgins that Jesus gave in Matthew 25.

Jesus explained that a master gave one slave five talents, a second slave two talents, and a third slave one talent. The master then went away, but *"after a long time the master of those slaves came and settled accounts with them"* (Matt. 25:19). The time reference to *"a long time"* is relevant because this is very different than time references (within a generation) made earlier in the discourse about events very near to the time of the disciples. When the master did return he required each slave to give an accounting; then he rewarded or punished them individually according to what they had done with their talents.

Similarly, we see a lapse of time when the ten virgins are waiting for the bridegroom. Enough time lapsed for five of the virgins to run out of oil for their lamps. As a result, they were not allowed entrance into the marriage feast. This fits well with the first century Jewish customs of marriage. After a man and woman were engaged, the man was required to go away and work until he could earn enough money and prepare a place for her. Only after he was ready to take care of her was he allowed to return to his fiancee and take her to the marriage feast. Hence, we see the marriage of Jesus with His Bride taking place at the end of this age, before the Messianic Age.

Earlier we explained how partial preterists have varying views on what part of Matthew 24 and 25 will be fulfilled in the future. As a partial preterist (who is also a historical preterist), I have explained Matthew 25 as happening in the future. Some partial preterists would offer some variations on this, but all partial preterists agree that Jesus will return in the future, and that event is often referred to as the Second Coming of Jesus—an event so foundational to orthodox Christianity that it is worth further clarification.

Chapter 7
His Second Coming?

Partial preterists (both historical and modern) look for a future day when Jesus will return and judge all of humanity. In contrast, full preterists do not believe Jesus will come back or there will be a future day of judgment. Adherents of full preterism believe those events happened in A.D. 70.

Christians who believe in a future return of Jesus typically refer to that day as the Second Coming. However, that terminology is not used anywhere in the Bible. This does not mean it is wrong to refer to it as the Second Coming, but that terminology can be confusing when we are a studying this subject from a theological perspective. We already mentioned how Jesus came the first time when He was born in Bethlehem. The Bible also refers to Jesus' enthronement in Heaven as a coming. Then Jesus came in power in A.D. 70 to judge Jerusalem. Therefore, if we are going to be theologically accurate, we would have to refer to any coming of Jesus after A.D. 70 as His fourth coming, fifth coming, or some additional coming.

These multiple comings are difficult for some Christians to envision because they have become comfortable using the label Second Coming to refer to the day in the future when Jesus returns. In reality, the word *coming* (*parousia* in Greek) was a common word in Bible days. The word is used 24 times in the New Testament:

- 1 Corinthians 16:17 refers to the coming of Stephanas, Fortunatus, and Achaicus
- 2 Corinthians 7:6-7 refer to Titus' coming
- 2 Corinthians 10:10, Philippians 1:26 and 2:12 talk about Paul's coming, but some Bible translations refer to Paul's coming as his *appearing*
- 2 Thessalonians 2:8-9 tells us about the coming of the lawless one
- 2 Peter 3:12 speaks of the coming of the Day of God;
- Plus there are 17 other places that use this word *coming*, referring to the coming of Jesus

The point is that the Greek word *parousia* was used in everyday language during New Testament times.

In order to understand how words are used in the Bible, it is important that readers know how common words can take on new meaning when they are used in a specific manner over and over again. For example, the word *gay* was a common word used for several hundred years by English-speaking people, and it meant "happy" or "joyful." However, the homosexual community has used the word to refer to themselves so many times that now when people hear the word *gay* they think of homosexuality.

In a comparative way, we can see how a common word such as *coming* has been used by Christians who focus on the Second Coming of Jesus. In reality, the word *coming* (*parousia* in Greek) was commonly used in the New Testament, and some of those times have nothing to do with Jesus or His coming.

We can also consider the Greek word *eisodos*, which is also translated in the New Testament as "coming" or "arrival." For example, Acts 13:23-24 refers to Jesus' coming as He stepped out to begin His public ministry:

> *according to promise, God has brought to Israel a Savior, Jesus, after John had proclaimed before His coming*

[eisodos] *a baptism of repentance to all the people of Israel.*

Hebrew 10:19 refers to our entrance boldly before God:

> *Therefore, brethren, since we have confidence to enter* [ei-sodos] *the holy place by the blood of Jesus.*

Parousia and *eisodos* were common words used in everyday language in Bible times. We must know this if we are going to understand the meaning of such words as they were used in Bible times.

This is important because full preterists seize the word *parousia,* and restrict its meaning to a onetime event that they believe happened in A.D. 70.

Such seizure of a word is especially easy when using a word of a different language that is unfamiliar to the audience. The person wielding the foreign word can tell the audience whatever he wants about the meaning of that word. Plus a foreign word has a mysterious attribute that leaves the untrained in a disadvantaged position.

For example, a medical doctor may tell a patient that she has *acute paronychia.* If the patient has no medical training, this diagnosis may instill within her fear and serious concerns. If she tries to go about her daily business without learning what this diagnosis means, she may be paralyzed as she tries to accomplish her routine tasks. On the other hand, if she is familiar with medical terms, she will immediately know that *acute paronychia* simply refers to the infection of a hangnail.

I say this to put the word *coming* back into the hands of normal everyday use. The word *coming* was much more common than the word *hangnail.*

Full preterists prefer to call the coming of Jesus "The Parousia." Using the Greek word and setting it apart by capitalizing it takes one's understanding out of everyday language and leads readers to envision some grand event that deserves this title. Then the reader is made to think there can only be one such grand event. With only one grand event called "The Parousia," full preterists place it at A.D. 70.

This manner of communication is deceptive, but it is common in the writings of full preterists. For example, James Stuart Russell,[11] whom full preterists consider one of their greatest champions, actually named his most famous book, *The Parousia.* In his book, Russell wrote:

> *The same event cannot be imminent at two different periods separated by nearly two thousand years.*[12]

Russel is right that the same event cannot happen at two different times, but that is the whole point. The only reason full preterists see "The Parousia" as one event is because they have taken the Greek word *parousia* and exulted it far beyond its biblical meaning.

Paul had more than one *parousia* (2 Cor. 10:10; Phil. 1:26; 2:12), and so can Jesus.

We already discussed several different comings of Jesus. We saw His coming as a baby, His coming into His ministry (Acts 13:23-24), and His coming before the Ancient of Days to receive His Kingdom (Chapter 3). Interestingly, Peter referred to Jesus' manifestation in glory on the Mount of Transfiguration (Matt. 17:1-9) as a coming (*parousia*) (2 Peter 1:16-18).[13] We also identified Jesus' coming (*parousia*) in power to judge Jerusalem in A.D. 70. Then we identified Jesus' future coming (*parousia*), when He will return in glory with His angels to judge all the nations of the world. So far we have six comings of Jesus talked about in the New Testament.

1. Coming as a baby (4 B.C.);
2. Coming into His ministry (A.D. 27);
3. Coming before the Father to receive His Kingdom (A.D. 30);

---

11 Some full preterists do not consider Russell a true full preterist because Russell sees Revelation 20:5-10 as still unfulfilled.

12 James Stuart Russel, *The Parousia* (Bradford, PA: International Preterist Association, 2003), p. xxix.

13 Some Bible teachers say 2 Peter 1:16-18 is referring to Jesus first coming, but either way the Greek word *parousia* is being used to refer to a coming of Jesus separate from A.D. 70.

4. Coming on the Mount of Transfiguration (A.D. 29 or 30);

5. Coming to destroy Jerusalem (A.D. 70);

6. Coming in glory to judge the nations of the world (future).

We can see another coming of Jesus, which Paul wrote about in 2 Thessalonians 2:8-9. In this passage, Paul talks about the *parousia* of Jesus and the *parousia* of the lawless one:

> *Then that lawless one will be revealed whom the Lord will slay with the breath of His mouth and bring to an end by the appearance of His coming* [parousia]; *that is, the one whose coming* [parousia] *is in accord with the activity of Satan....*

According to this passage, the lawless one will be destroyed at the *parousia* of Jesus.

Full preterists only believe in one *parousia,* which happened by A.D. 70, so this forces them to identify "the lawless one" as some leader who lived around A.D. 70. Many full preterists have decided the lawless one was Nero, the emperor of the Roman Empire from A.D. 54 to 68.[14] Knowing the *parousia* of Jesus must slay the lawless one and knowing Nero committed suicide in A.D. 68, full preterists must see our Lord's *parousia* at A.D. 68. This marks the seventh coming of Jesus:[15]

7. Coming to destroy the lawless one (A.D. 68).

Full preterists who see Nero as the lawless one have a problem here because Jesus must have a *parousia* to correspond with the death of Nero in A.D. 68; plus they have the judgment of Jerusalem in A.D. 70. They solve their problem by expanding their definition of "The Parousia" to extend over a longer period of time, which includes both the A.D. 68 and 70 judgments. Similarly, when full preterists read about Jesus' *parousia* on the

---

14 Some identify the lawless one as John Levi or some other leader who was alive during the first century.

15 Full preterists who associate the lawless one as John Levi do not have this problem because John probably died in A.D. 70 at the Jerusalem destruction.

Mount of Transfiguration, they have to expand their definition of "The Parousia" from A.D. 30 to 70.

Rather than expand our definition of "The Parousia," it is more natural to simply recognize the Greek word as a common word that simply means "coming." Then we can see that Jesus can come and manifest His Kingdom, power, and glory whenever He wants as often as He wants—including our future.

Full preterists may object and say if that is true, then we have no way of knowing the timing of any one coming mentioned in Scripture. But that is the point. Once we abandon the false grandeur built up around the Greek word *parousia*, then we can read the context of each passage and determine what coming is being referred to in that passage. We do not have to force each coming into one predetermined date. We can let the Bible speak for itself.

For example, we can read about the occasion when Paul preached in Greece to the Athenians. He declared:

> *...He* [God] *has fixed **a day in which He will judge the world** in righteousness through a Man* [Jesus] *whom He has appointed, having furnished proof to all men by raising Him from the dead.*
>
> (Acts 17:31)

This declaration was made at the end of Paul's speech as the culmination of all he told the Athenians. Paul was teaching about the coming judgment of *"the world"* as a warning to his audience that they needed to repent and live righteously.

Full preterists insist that the day of judgment, of which Paul was warning them, happened in A.D. 70 at the fall of Jerusalem, but that is nonsensical. A judgment that was supposed to happen in a distant city to a foreign people would have been of little concern to those Gentile Athenians—certainly no reason for them to repent.

Furthermore, Paul stated that the coming judgment would be of the world, and the Greek word used here is *oikoumene*, which literally means "civilized world" and was used at that time in history to refer to the Roman Empire.

If anyone reads Acts 17:31 without the presupposition of the A.D. 70 date, they would conclude Jesus was appointed by God to judge the world, a judgment that would include the Gentiles living in Greece. The judgment of Jerusalem did not include the Greeks. So we must look for another date when the world is judged.

There are many Bible verses that talk about a future coming of Jesus and His judgment of the whole world. Full preterists explain these as having happened in A.D. 70, but partial preterists and almost all Christians hold the following verses to be about a future return of Jesus.

and that He may send Jesus, the Christ appointed for you, whom Heaven must receive until the period of restoration of all things about which God spoke by the mouth of His holy prophets from ancient time.

(Acts 3:20-21)

For as often as you eat this bread and drink the cup, you proclaim the Lord's death until He comes.

(1 Cor. 11:26)

But each in his own order: Christ the first fruits, after that those who are Christ's at His coming, then comes the end, when He hands over the kingdom to the God and Father, when He has abolished all rule and all authority and power.

(1 Cor. 15:23-24)

For our citizenship is in Heaven, from which also we eagerly wait for a Savior, the Lord Jesus Christ;

(Phil. 3:20)

so that He may establish your hearts without blame in holiness before our God and Father at the coming of our Lord Jesus with all His saints.

(1 Thes. 3:13)

For if we believe that Jesus died and rose again, even so God will bring with Him those who have fallen asleep in Jesus. For this we say to you by the word of the Lord, that we who are alive and remain until the coming of the Lord, will not precede those who have fallen asleep. For the Lord Himself will descend from Heaven with a shout, with the voice of the archangel and with the trumpet of God, and the dead in Christ will rise first. Then we who are alive and remain will be caught up together with them in the clouds to meet the Lord in the air, and so we shall always be with the Lord.

(1 Thes. 4:14-17)

when the Lord Jesus will be revealed from heaven with His mighty angels in flaming fire, dealing out retribution to those who do not know God and to those who do not obey the gospel of our Lord Jesus.

(2 Thes. 1:7-8)

I solemnly charge you in the presence of God and of Christ Jesus, who is to judge the living and the dead, and by His appearing and His kingdom.

(2 Tim. 4:1)

looking for the blessed hope and the appearing of the glory of our great God and Savior, Christ Jesus,

(Titus 2:13)

so Christ also, having been offered once to bear the sins of many, will appear a second time for salvation without reference to sin, to those who eagerly await Him.

(Heb. 9:28)

These are only a few of the many verses that speak of Jesus coming back at some point in the future.

Chapter 8
All Things Fulfilled?

Full preterists hold that everything God promised in the Bible has been accomplished. To support their belief that all prophecies were fulfilled by A.D. 70, full preterists often quote Luke 21:20-22:

> But when you see Jerusalem surrounded by armies, then recognize that her desolation is near...these are days of vengeance, so that **all things which are written will be fulfilled**.

According to full preterists, these verses prove that everything written in the Bible was fulfilled by A.D. 70. Since that date there has been nothing more that God has had to do in the world. It would be difficult to overemphasize how much full preterists build their arguments based on this Bible passage.

In reality, full preterists read Luke 21:20-22 through their own worldview. To see this, note how Luke uses the same terminology, *"all things which were written,"* just two chapters prior to the passage in Luke 21:

> Then He took the twelve aside and said to them, "Behold, we are going up to Jerusalem, and **all things which are written** through the prophets about the Son of Man will be accomplished. For He will be handed over to the Gen-

> *tiles, and will be mocked and mistreated and spit upon,*
> *and after they have scourged Him, they will kill Him;*
> *and the third day He will rise again."*
>
> (Luke 18:31-33)

In these verses, Luke quotes Jesus as referring to all things written being accomplished as they were about to make their last trip to Jerusalem. However, we know that all things written about Jesus were not accomplished at that time. For example, we know that His judgment of Jerusalem was not going to happen until A.D. 70.

This does not mean Jesus or Luke were wrong. It simply means we have to reconsider how we understand the phrase, *"all things which were written."* We must understand this phrase within its context.

In the context of Luke 18:31-33, Jesus was referring to all things written concerning His death and resurrection. All those things were fulfilled when they went into Jerusalem in A.D. 30. Similarly, in Luke 21:20-22, when Jesus referred to all things written, the context was concerning the destruction of Jerusalem. All things written about that destruction were fulfilled in A.D. 70.

Luke used similar terminology as he recorded Paul's teaching in Acts 13:

> *When they had **carried out all that was written concerning Him**, they took Him down from the cross and laid Him in a tomb.*
>
> (Acts 13:29)

Notice that in this verse Luke refers to all that was written about Jesus being fulfilled when Jesus died. Yet, we know the Scriptures tell us of other things Jesus accomplished after His death, such as ascending into Heaven, sitting at the right hand of God, and judging humanity. Obviously, *"all things written"* did not refer to all things written in the whole Bible.

It only makes sense to understand the phrase *"all things writ-ten"* within the context it is used. In Acts 13:29, Luke was re-ferring to all things written about Jesus' death being fulfilled when He died. Similarly, Luke 21:20-22 tells us all things writ-ten about the destruction of Jerusalem were, indeed, fulfilled in A.D. 70.

Yet, full preterists will not accept this explanation. They cling to their understanding that all things written throughout the whole Bible were fulfilled in A.D. 70.

To see that the full preterist's understanding of Luke 21:20-22 is wrong, all we have to do is find one verse in the Bible that has not yet been fulfilled. However, if we find a verse, full pret-erists will try to find some way to explain it as having already been fulfilled. Yet, there are some verses that are very difficult to explain away. For example, most Christians will agree that the following promises of God were not fulfilled by A.D. 70 and they still have not been fulfilled today:

> *The scepter will not depart from Judah, nor the ruler's staff from between his feet, until he comes to whom it belongs and **the obedience of the nations is his**.*
> (Gen. 49:10, NIV)

> ***Nations will come to your light**,*
> *And kings to the brightness of your rising.*
> (Is. 60:3)

Anyone, except full preterists, will admit the nations of the Earth have not yet come to Jesus or to the glory of God. Full preterists redefine and spiritualize promises such as these to make them fit into their A.D. 70 timetable. Then they can claim their viewpoint is consistent—hence, calling their own view "consistent preterism" or "consistent eschatology." Once full preterists have succeeded in explaining all of God's promises as fulfilled, then they can accuse anyone who rejects their expla-nations as being inconsistent with Luke 21:20-22.

In reality, full preterists are misinterpreting Luke 21:20-22.

Not only is Luke 21:20-22 referring to all of the Scriptures about the destruction being fulfilled, but we also should note the verb tenses in these verses:

> *But when you see Jerusalem surrounded by armies, then recognize that her desolation is near...these are days of vengeance, so that all things which are written **will be fulfilled**.*

This verse is explaining that certain events had to happen so that other events *will* happen. The King James Version words this as *"all things which are written may be fulfilled."* Either translation gives the idea, which is in the original Greek, that one event (destruction of Jerusalem) happened so that other events will happen for the fulfillment of all that is written in Scripture.

We can compare this to a man named Ray who purchased a car, so he can drive across the country. Ray already purchased the car, but he has not yet driven across the country. In a comparative way, Jerusalem was destroyed and a new Kingdom was established so that *"all things which are written will be fulfilled."*

What we are saying is that the verb tenses used in Luke 21:22 do not imply that all things written were fulfilled by A.D. 70.

This is very important in the debate between partial and full preterists, because full preterists base their eschatology upon the idea that all prophecies in the Bible had to have been fulfilled by A.D. 70. That date is the anchor point for all their interpretations.

Next we will see how that anchor point molds their understanding of the Book of Revelation.

Chapter 9
Revelation Events Are Near

Now we can talk about the Book of Revelation and consider if the full preterists are correct in saying the entire Book was fulfilled by A.D. 70.

Their primary argument is centered around the time references in the text itself. Jesus began the Revelation by saying He was going to reveal *"things which must soon take place"* (Rev. 1:1). Jesus reemphasized this by saying, *"the time is near"* (Rev. 1:3). In the last chapter of the Revelation, an angel referred to *"things which must soon take place"* (Rev. 22:6) and *"the time is near"* (Rev. 22:10). Full preterists understand these time references to mean that events of the Book of Revelation were fulfilled by A.D. 70.[16]

The error full preterists make is in equating two different phrases:

"things which must soon **take place**"
"things which must soon **be fulfilled**"

This distinction becomes clear when we consider events in the Book of Revelation that have not yet been fulfilled even today. For example, Revelation 11:15 says:

The kingdom of the world has become the kingdom of our Lord and of His Christ; and He will reign forever and ever.

---

16 Partial and full preterists agree the Book of Revelation was written before A.D. 70. For an explanation of this dating, see *Victorious Eschatology.*

The first part of this verse—the kingdom of world has become the kingdom of our Lord—has been fulfilled. However, the second part—He will reign forever and ever—has not been fulfilled. Any logical person realizes this verse can never be fulfilled as long as time governs this world. The Kingdom of God was near in the first century, but the ongoing reign of Jesus continues today.

We can compare this to the founding of the United States as an independent country. In 1776, the citizens of the colonies fought Britain for their freedom. When the war started their leaders could say, "Freedom is near!" Indeed, the people of the United States were victorious, and the United States was established. However, the United States still exists today as an independent country.

In a comparative way, we can say the events recorded in Revelation were near in the first century when Jesus revealed them to John. That meant the events recorded in Revelation were soon to begin unfolding. Or we can say the events began to commence. However, this does not mean all events were fulfilled.

Consider Revelation 20:10, which tells us the beast and false prophet are thrown into the Lake of Fire and *"they will be tormented day and night forever and ever."* There is a point in time when this torment must begin, but it can never be fulfilled in the sense of being completed.

Full preterists may object and say such references to *forever and ever* should not be included in this discussion, but they have to be included because we are trying to determine the meaning of the time-reference phrases used in the Book of Revelation, such as, *"things which must soon take place"* (Rev. 1:1) and *"the time is near"* (Rev. 1:3). The events in the Book of Revelation that will go on forever and ever *prove* the time-reference phrases were indicative of events that began to unfold in the first century but were not necessarily fulfilled.

Full preterists often misquote Revelation 1:1, referring to, "things which must soon be *fulfilled*." In reality, the word, *fulfilled* is not there, but full preterists often misquote this verse, which causes inattentive listeners to believe all of the events of Revelation were fulfilled.

Christians who are diligent in their study of the Bible try hard to read the Bible independently of their own biases. One way to identify one's own biases is to take note of where one consciously and unconsciously adds or changes words in the text. Those added words make subtle changes in line with what a person wants the Bible to say. Christians who want to identify their own biases will immediately reconsider their understanding of Revelation 1:1 the instant someone points out how they added a word that was not in the original text.

The context of Revelation 1 actually reveals that the events would *not* all be fulfilled soon. Jesus said that He would reveal *"things which must soon take place"* (Rev. 1:1), however, in the same chapter, Jesus told John to:

> *write the things which you have seen, and the things which are, and the things which will take place after these things.*
>
> (Rev. 1:19)

There is a sequence of events mentioned in this verse. So then, we can say the events foreseen in vision by John began to unfold in John's lifetime, but some events were to be later down in the sequence of events.

Finally, consider Revelation 15:4, which says, *"For all the nations will come and worship before You..."* It would be difficult to say this actually happened before Jerusalem was destroyed in A.D. 70.

Once we have some measure of confidence that some events recorded in Revelation take place after A.D. 70, we can delve into the Book to see what those events are.

Chapter 10
Reading the Revelation

Generally speaking, partial and full preterists agree about the first 5 chapters of the Book of Revelation. Chapter 1 is an introduction, talking about John's encounter with Jesus. Chapters 2-3 are seven letters addressed to seven churches that existed in the first century. In Revelation 4-5, the apostle John is taken to Heaven where he sees what is taking place in the throneroom of God.

It is the rest of the Book at which we need to take a closer look. In order to give this subject the attention it deserves, we need to discuss individually the main sections:

Revelation 6-11:	First set of judgments
Revelation 12-18:	Second set of judgments[17]
Revelation 19:	Return of Jesus
Revelation 19:	Marriage feast
Revelation 20:	Millennium
Revelation 20:	Great White Throne Judgment
Revelation 21-22:	Creation of the new Heaven and Earth

Partial and full preterists agree about the first set of judgments, which are described in Revelation 6 to 11. Those chapters are referring to the judgment of Israel, including the destruction of Jerusalem and the Temple.

For those who have not been exposed to the partial or full

---

17 Some Bible teachers break these into more than two sets of judgments.

preterists' understanding of Revelation 6 to 11, a few words of explanation will be helpful. In chapter 6, we see Jesus beginning to break the seals that release the angels for war. In chapter 7, we see angels sealing 144,000 sons of Israel so they will be spared from the imminent judgment. Then in chapters 8 to 11 destruction is released upon Israel, which was fulfilled in A.D. 70.

Several references in Revelation 6 to 11 lead the reader to believe these chapters are about the destruction of Israel. For example, there is a clear reference to Jerusalem in Revelation 11:8:

> ...*the great city which mystically is called Sodom and Egypt, where also their Lord was crucified.*

There is only one city where the Lord was crucified—Jerusalem. Plus there are several other Bible passages that associate Jerusalem with Sodom (Deut. 32:32; Is. 1:9-10; Jer. 23:14; Ez. 16:48-49, 53). In chapter 11, we also see John measuring the Temple in Jerusalem (11:1), and then it is destroyed (11:2), but a new Temple in Heaven is opened (11:19). These are a few of the references that lead partial and full preterists to conclude that Revelation 6 to 11 were fulfilled when Jerusalem was destroyed.

It is the rest of the Book of Revelation over which partial and full preterists disagree. We will see their disagreements over the following:

Revelation 12-18:	Second set of judgments
Revelation 19:	Return of Jesus
Revelation 19:	Marriage feast
Revelation 20:	Millennium
Revelation 20:	Great White Throne Judgment
Revelation 21-22:	Creation of the new Heaven and Earth

As a partial preterist (who is a historical preterist), I see the events listed above happening in the order in which they are given in the Book of Revelation. For example, I see the marriage feast (which is talked about in Revelation 19) happening before the Millennium (which is talked about in Revelation 20).

Partial Preterist Reading of the Book of Revelation

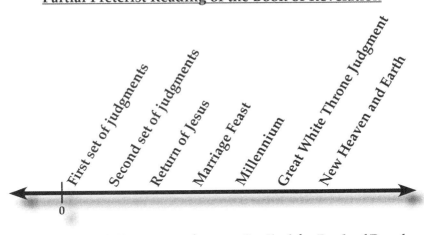

In contrast, full preterists have to fit all of the Book of Revelation before the end of A.D. 70. Therefore, they have to interpret the Book as if it is reporting about the same period of time over and over.

Full Preterist Reading the Book of Revelation

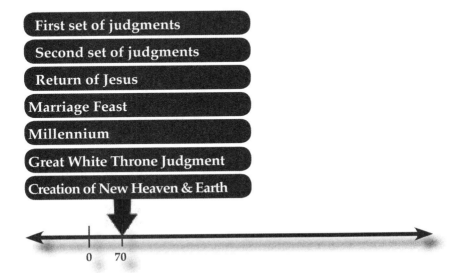

James Stuart Russell, who is greatly admired by full preterists,[18] explained this, saying the Book of Revelation:

> *is not a continuous and progressive sequence of events, but a continually recurring representation of substantially the same tragic history in fresh forms and new phases.*[19]

To see this full preterist understanding, consider how the first set of judgments in chapters 6 to 11 ended with the destruction of the Temple. Full preterists cannot allow any events to occur after that destruction, so they must see the second set of judgments (chapter 12 to 18) as a repeat of that destruction. Then the return of Jesus and the marriage feast talked about in Revelation 19 also have to fit into the same time period. Then the Millennium in chapter 20 has to fit. Then the Great White Throne Judgment has to happen during the same period. And finally the creation of the new Heaven and Earth has to happen during the same period before the end of A.D. 70.

Full preterists have a difficult time seeing their own inconsistency in this view of the Book of Revelation, yet it is obvious to those who do not embrace it. Full preterists read all of the events that happen within any one section as happening sequentially, but then they break that sequence when it fits their presuppositions. For example, full preterists read Revelation chapters 6 to 11 as if John is reporting sequential events. Then when John starts chapter 12, they say he is starting over. When full preterists read chapters 12 to 18, they say John is reporting sequential events, but when they hit Revelation 19, they say John is starting over. When full preterists read Revelation 20, they say John is reporting sequential events throughout chapter 20, but when they start Revelation chapter 21, they say John is starting over. Each of these starting over points just happens to match the full preterists' presuppositions which correspond to

---

18 Although Russell is admired, some full preterists do not consider Russell a true full preterist because Russell sees Revelation 20:5-10 as still unfulfilled.

19 James Stuart Russell, *The Parousia* (Bradford, PA: International Preterist Association, 2003), p. 406.

their belief that all events must fit before A.D. 70.

Of course, this way of reading the Book of Revelations seems natural to full preterists. Anyone who looks at a passage the same way over and over again will eventually see it as natural. Also, when people read a passage through their own world-view they will see it as natural.

However, it is much more natural to read the Book of Revelation without the chapter breaks that were not in John's initial writings. As every Bible teacher knows, those chapter breaks were added so people can refer to specific passages more easily. Anyone who reads the whole Book of Revelation from start to finish without those chapter breaks is more likely to see it as reporting a sequence of events, Revelation chapters 1 to 22.

Chapter 11
Second Set of Judgments[20]

Partial and full preterists agree that the judgments talked about in Revelation 6 to 11 are about the judgment of the Jewish religious leaders and Jerusalem. However, we need to take a closer look at the judgments talked about in chapters 12 to 18. This second set of judgments is revealed as different from the earlier set of judgments. There is a different set of angels administering judgments in entirely different ways (pouring out the seven bowls of the wrath of God). We need to identify who this second set of judgments was directed toward.

Because full preterists see all of the Book of Revelation fulfilled by A.D. 70, they must see the judgments in chapters 12 to 18 as a repeat of the judgments in chapters 6 to 11. They must see both sets of judgments as directed toward the Jews and Jerusalem.

Some partial preterists (modern preterists) agree with full preterists that the second set of judgments overlap the first set and, hence, are directed toward the Jews and Jerusalem. Although I understand and respect the reasoning that has led some of my partial preterist friends to come to this conclusion, it seems to me that the second set of judgments is not directed toward the Jews and Jerusalem.

I do not want to make a big issue about this, because you can believe either view and still be a partial preterist. In the rest of

---

20 Some Bible teachers break these into more than two sets of judgments.

this chapter I will offer my understanding concerning the second set of judgments. If this is a non-issue for you, please jump to the next chapter, where I continue addressing the primary message of this book which is to contrast the partial and full preterist views.

As a partial preterist (historical preterist), I can point out several verses in the Bible that indicate God intended to judge more than the Jews after the Kingdom was established. We know the Jews had to be judged first because we are told:

> *There will be tribulation and distress for every soul of man who does evil, of the Jew first and also of the Greek,*
> (Rom. 2:9)

After the judgment of the Jews, Paul referred to judgment coming upon the Greeks. For Paul, the Greeks were not the same as the Gentiles. He used the term *Gentile* to refer to anyone who was non-Jewish, while the term *Greeks* referred to the inhabitants of the Roman Empire.

We know the Roman Empire had to be judged, because Daniel interpreted a dream of King Nebuchadnezzar and explained from that dream how God was going to set up His Kingdom on Earth during the Roman Empire, causing that Empire to crumble (Dan. 2:40-45).

The judgment of the Roman Empire is no small issue in the Bible. Both the Old Testament and New Testament state it clearly. Here we need to see it in the Book of Revelation. We do not need to give a verse-by-verse study of the Book of Revelation (that study you can get in *Victorious Eschatology*), but there are several images in Revelation 12 to 18 that support the idea that the Roman Empire was on the receiving end of God's judgments.

One way to see this is to study the 144,00[21] people who were sealed before each set of judgments. The sealing of 144,000 happened twice. In Revelation 7, before the first set of judgments

---

21 Neither partial nor full preterists take this number literally but understand it in the Hebrew context that God was marking a large remnant, sufficient to satisfy His desire to spare a remnant from the judgments.

were released, God had 144,000 from the *"sons of Israel"* sealed (7:4). In Revelation 14, before the second set of judgments were released, God had 144,000 Christians sealed (*"having His name and the name of His Father written on their foreheads"*—14:1). It seems to me that God had sons of Israel sealed in Revelation 7, because His first set of judgments was directed toward the Jews. God had Christians sealed before the second set of judgments because that set of judgments was directed toward the region where most Christians lived, i.e., the Roman Empire.

Full preterists cannot allow Revelation 12 to 18 to speak of the judgment of the Roman Empire. The city of Rome was destroyed in A.D. 410, while the whole Empire collapsed in A.D. 476. These late dates are incompatible with full preterism. If full preterists allow Revelation 12 to 18 to be about events that happened as late as A.D. 476, then the events of Revelation 19 to 22 may also happen after A.D. 70. Full preterists cannot allow that because it opens the door for a future return of Jesus, marriage feast, Millennium, Great White Throne Judgment, and new Heaven and Earth. That would cause the entire position of full preterism to crumble. They have no wiggle room on this issue. If they pull the anchor of A.D. 70, their whole system of thought goes down the drain.

Yet, if people study the Book of Revelation without the preconceived idea that it must all be fulfilled by A.D. 70, they will conclude that many reported events are fulfilled after A.D. 70. This becomes evident when we study the descriptions of the harlot and Babylon in the Revelation. The harlot/Babylon are prominent in these chapters, and they are the primary target of the second set of judgments.

Full preterists claim the harlot/Babylon is Jerusalem, and therefore, chapters 12 to 18 of Revelation are reporting judgments against Jerusalem. Their arguments for equating Jerusalem with Babylon are feeble at best. First, they read Revelation 11:8, which says:

> ...*the great city which mystically is called Sodom and Egypt, where also their Lord was crucified.*

We know this reference is to Jerusalem, because Jesus was crucified in Jerusalem. Full preterists go on to note that Jerusalem is called the "great city"; then they note that the harlot is also called a "great city" in Revelation 17:18. Since both are called "great cities," full preterists equate the two.

In reality, simply referring to two cities as *great* does not make them the same city. The Greek word for *great* is *megas,* which a common adjective that can be used to describe any large city. Today we can say that New York is a large city, and we can also say that London is large city, but just because they are both large cities does not mean they are the same.

Furthermore, we know the two great cities, Jerusalem and Babylon, are *not* the same because of the gender references. When the Book of Revelation refers to Jerusalem (Rev. 11:8), the original Greek uses the male gender for both the noun, *city,* and the adjective, *great (polous megalēs).* When referring to the other city called the harlot/Babylon, the original Greek uses the female gender for both the noun, *city* and the adjective, *great (polis megalē).* This alone is enough to let the reader know that these are two different cities. In the Book of Revelation, the harlot/Babylon is not Jerusalem.

The description of the harlot/Babylon in the book of Revelation does even not match Jerusalem. Revelation 17:18 says the harlot *"reigns over the kings of the earth."* This does not fit Jerusalem. Jerusalem had been subjected to other rulers for over 400 years. When the Book of Revelation was written, Jerusalem was under occupation by Roman soldiers and government leaders.

Revelation 16:19 tells us that when the harlot was destroyed, *"the cities of the nations fell."* Jerusalem was not so important that when it was destroyed, *"the cities of the nations fell."*

On the other hand, the city of Rome does fit the description of the great city. At that time in history, Rome was the center of the Empire. The Caesars at Rome were positioned over the kings of Earth, and all of the nations were under Rome's influence. When Rome fell in A.D. 410, every city of the nations was dramatically impacted.

Furthermore, John told us the harlot sits on seven mountains (Rev. 17:9). In the same context, he said those seven mountains are seven kings. This is similar language to that used earlier to describe Rome (Rev. 12:3) and the seven Caesars that ruled the Roman Empire. Not only did the Roman Empire have seven Caesars, but the city of Rome was surrounded by seven mountains.

Full preterists try to convince people that Jerusalem was surrounded by seven mountains, but no where in ancient history do we have records of Jerusalem being associated with seven mountains. At the same time, Rome was widely known as "The City on Seven Hills" (in antiquity, called *Septimontium*). The first century Jewish readers of the Book of Revelation would have known this and, therefore, equated The City on Seven Hills with Rome.

To see the connection between Babylon and Rome we need to consider the history of the people surrounding Israel. In ancient times, there were four mighty people groups who dominated the region around the Mediterranean Sea: the Babylonians, the Medo-Persians, the Greeks, and the Romans. To the Jews, those people groups were often lumped together as the heathen, the oppressors, even the dogs. The authority over the region had simply been passed from one group to another: from the Babylonians, to the Medo-Persians, to the Greeks, to the Romans. To the Jews, they were all oppressors—the enemies of God's people.

More significantly, Babylon was known among the Jews as the city and kingdom that destroyed Jerusalem and the Temple the first time. In 425 B.C., Nebuchadnezzar began a war against Jerusalem. After 30 months of starvation and diseases ravaging the people of Jerusalem, Nebuchadnezzar's soldiers breached the walls of Jerusalem. Almost one million Jews were murdered, buildings throughout the city were burned, and the Temple was destroyed. The Jews who survived the holocaust were taken out of the Promised Land as slaves.

It would be difficult to over-emphasize the significance of that Babylonian war against the Jews. When modern Christians first learn about the Roman war of A.D. 70, they are often shocked that no one had ever told them about this historical event. Similarly, when it comes to the Babylonian war of 425 B.C., Christians rarely have an awareness of how central it was (and still is) in Jewish history and the Bible. The Temple Solomon built was destroyed. Jewish life was centered around that Temple and the religious rituals that were practiced there. The ark of the tabernacle, which represented the presence and blessing of God, was lost. The Jews felt God had abandoned them.

Much of the material in the Old Testament that is accredited to the major and minor prophets focuses on the Babylonian war with Jerusalem. That destruction is most clearly described by Jeremiah in the Book of Lamentations. Even today the Babylonian destruction is so central to Jewish thought that the Book of Lamentations is read in the synagogue every year on the eve of the Ninth of Av in remembrance of what took place when Jerusalem and the first Temple were destroyed.

When first-century Jews thought of Babylon, they thought of their own destruction in the fifth century B.C. Hence, we can know that Babylon does not refer to Jerusalem. It referred to the enemy of Jerusalem.

The Four Ruling Groups around the Mediterranean Sea

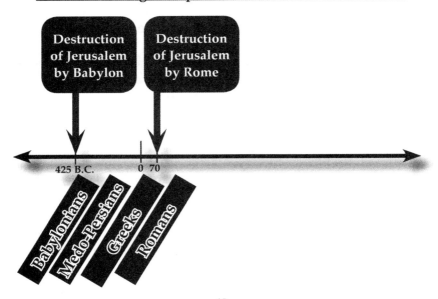

Babylon destroyed Jerusalem and the Temple the first time; Rome destroyed Jerusalem and the Temple the second time.

We must read the Book of Revelation with this in mind. John was primarily writing to Jews who had become Christians. They were under terrible persecution by the Roman Empire. If John had referred directly to Rome when he wrote the Book of Revelation, anyone caught with a copy would have been punished severely. Babylon was the closest association the Jewish people had to Rome.

To confirm that the harlot/Babylon referred to Rome, consider Revelation 17:6, which describes the harlot:

*And I saw the woman drunk with the blood of the saints,
and with the blood of the witnesses of Jesus.*

Full preterists like to quote this verse, then say that the Jews were the ones who were drunk with the blood of the saints. Then full preterists can lead their audience to conclude that the harlot/Babylon was Jerusalem.

A little study reveals something different. When Jesus declared the destruction of Jerusalem (Matt. 23), He said *"the guilt of all the righteous blood shed on earth, from the blood of righteous Abel to the blood of Zechariah"* was to fall upon the Jewish religious leaders (vs. 35). Those are Old Testament saints.

In contrast, Revelation 17:6 speaks of *"the blood of the witnesses of Jesus."* These are New Testament saints.

It was Rome where the vast majority of Christians were killed. In fact, it was illegal for the Jews to put anyone to death while they were under Roman rule (John 18:31). At times mobs got out of control and stoned someone (e.g., Acts 7:58-59), but the only way for Jews to legally have someone put to death was to go through the Roman legal system.

Jews were not even involved in most of the killing of Christians. Emperor Nero blamed the burning of the city of Rome in A.D. 64 on the Christians, which began a horrific period of Christian persecution. The historian, Tacitus (ca. A.D. 55-120), wrote how Christians were tortured, nailed to crosses, or covered in animal skins and then torn to death by dogs. The second major persecution took place during Domitian's reign (A.D. 81-96), when famine, pestilence, and earthquakes were blamed on Christians, leading to the martyrdom of untold numbers. Then the greatest and bloodiest persecution of Christians in the Roman Empire happened during the reign of Diocletian (A.D. 284 to 305), who became known in history as the "adversary of God." It was the city of Rome that was *"drunk with the blood of the saints, and with the blood of the witnesses of Jesus."*

All of these truths lead us to conclude that harlot/Babylon referred to Rome, not Jerusalem. Therefore, the second set of judgements described in Revelation 12-18, were against the Roman Empire, not the Jewish people.

Chapter 12
Covenant or Kingdom?

In the preceding chapter, I explained how partial preterists can be consistent and still believe the harlot/Babylon is Jerusalem or Rome. Either view is acceptable to partial preterists; however, which view is chosen correlates with a certain lens through which a person reads the Book of Revelation. This is a much more important issue.

The title of the Book of Revelation is actually the *Revelation of Jesus Christ*. From beginning to end the Book reveals Jesus as King. In Revelation 4, we see Jesus sitting on His throne after He ascended into Heaven. From chapters 4 to 18, judgments are released to destroy the enemies of King Jesus. Then in chapter 19, we see Jesus as totally victorious, reigning over His Kingdom.

Full preterists will give lip service to this understanding, and many honestly believe their view agrees with this explanation, but their view is actually very different. They primarily see the Book of Revelation as the destruction of the old covenant and its replacement with the new covenant. This lens of covenantal replacement is very different than the lens of King Jesus establishing His Kingdom.[22]

This distinction is key. You see, if Revelation 4 to 18 is about God's judgment against the old covenant, then it was fulfilled by A.D. 70. On the other hand, if Revelation 4 to 18 is about

---

22 Partial preterists who equate the harlot/Babylon with Jerusalem read the Book of Revelation through the same lens as full preterists.

the kingdoms of this world becoming the Kingdom of our God, then we do not have to limit our time frame to A.D. 70. The Kingdom of God was established when Jesus sat down at the right hand of God, and it will continue growing until every enemy is put under the feet of Jesus. That subduing of enemies goes beyond A.D. 70, because the Jews were not the only enemies of Jesus. Daniel (Dan. 2:40-45) and Paul (Rom. 2:9) told us the Roman Empire had to be judged. Both the Old Testament and New Testament tell us that every enemy of Jesus would be judged (Is. 9:6-7; 1 Cor. 15:25).

So what is the fundamental message of the Book of Revelation? Is Revelation about the obliteration of the old covenant and its replacement with the new? Or is it about establishing the Kingdom of God?

The truth is that neither the old covenant nor the new covenant is ever mentioned in the Book of Revelation—not once. In fact, the Revelation is one of the few books in the Bible in which the word *covenant* is never mentioned. In contrast, the words *King* and *Kingdom* are mentioned over 25 times in the Book, with dozens more references to these. Any one who reads the Book of Revelation without preconceived ideas will conclude that its primary message is about King Jesus and the Kingdom of God.

To see that the Book of Revelation is not fundamentally about the destruction of the old covenant, look more carefully at the old covenant. (We are referring to the Mosaic covenant, not the covenant God made with Abraham.) Paul wrote that Jesus:

> *abolished in His flesh the enmity, which is the Law of commandments...*
>
> (Eph. 2:15)

Paul gave further explanation in Colossians 2:14:

> *having canceled out the certificate of debt consisting of decrees against us, which was hostile to us; and He has taken it out of the way, having nailed it to the cross.*

Notice that the Law was "abolished" and "taken out of the way" at the death of Jesus.

The Old Covenant Was Abolished at the Death of Jesus

Why is this important? Because Jesus dealt with the old covenant in A.D. 30, long before the Book of Revelation was written.

Contrary to what full preterists would have us believe, God did not aim the judgments of Revelation 4 to 18 toward the old covenant. It did not take that much effort to eliminate it. God was not that mad at the old covenant. He did not need to kill 1.1 million Jews to obliterate the Mosaic religious system. The death of Jesus was enough. It required no more effort to destroy the old covenant.

Furthermore, the new covenant was established at the same time—when Jesus died. Our Lord told His disciples ahead of time, *"This is My blood of the covenant"* (Matt. 26:28). The writer of Hebrews explained that the new covenant was established with the death of Jesus (Heb. 9:15), the same instant the old covenant was made obsolete:

> *When He said, "A new covenant," He has made the first obsolete.*
>
> (Heb. 8:13)

The transition from the old to the new covenant happened in

A.D. 30., when Jesus took His last breath.

The New Covenant Was Established at the Death of Jesus

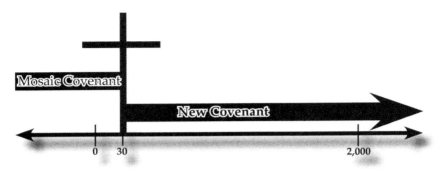

This is why it is wrong to interpret the Book of Revelation through the construct of seeing the old covenant destroyed and the new covenant established. Both of those events happened in A.D. 30, not A.D. 70.

Revelation 4 to 19 is not about destroying the old covenant, but it is about the kingdoms of this world becoming the Kingdom of Jesus. The events of A.D. 70 happened not because the old covenant still needed to be destroyed, but because the Jewish religious leaders were hardhearted and rejected Jesus as their King. King Jesus was punishing His enemies as He established His Kingdom. That was the reason Jerusalem was destroyed. It was Kingdom expansion, not old covenant demolition.

This Kingdom perspective also applies to Revelation 20 to 22. Full preterists see the creation of the new Heaven and Earth as the establishment of the new covenant, but the new covenant was fully established long before the Book of Revelation was written.

It is much more reasonable to understand Revelation 20 to 22 through the Jewish worldview of the first century. As we explained, the most common understanding of Jews in the first century was that God would send a messiah who would establish the Kingdom that was promised to King David, and that the Kingdom would grow until it brought in world peace and prosperity.

Most Common Jewish Eschatology in the First Century

Messiah Comes & Establishes His Kingdom

Messianic Age: Peace & Prosperity on Earth

The Jewish Christians who read the Book of Revelation during the first century would have understood the Book through their own worldview. This is it. It was a Kingdom worldview. They were looking for a King to set them free from the persecution and oppression they were experiencing. The Jewish Christians were looking for the Messiah to rule a Kingdom in righteousness, justice, and peace.

If modern Christians read the Book of the Revelation through the lens of covenant replacement, they will tend to see the judgments of Revelation 6 to 11 as directed toward the Jews and Jerusalem. They will also see the judgments of Revelation 12 to 18 as directed toward the Jews and Jerusalem. However, if Christians read the Book of Revelation through the eyes of the expanding Kingdom of God, they will see that the enemies of Jesus were being judged.

One of the reasons this distinction is important is because full preterists often defend their view by saying the subject matter of the Book of Revelation does not change: According to them, God is judging Jerusalem in Revelation 6 to 11, and

God is judging Jerusalem in Revelation 12 to 18. Full preterists point this out in order to contrast it with the partial preterist view that sees the first set of judgments against Jerusalem and the second set of judgments against Rome. Full preterists assert that God would not change the subject matter within the Book of Revelation.

In reality, the only reason full preterists see the partial preterists' view as changing the subject matter is because of the lens through which they are reading the Book of Revelation. They see the Book as primarily a report about the old covenant being replaced with the new covenant. As I have explained, the Book of Revelation is not about that. It is fundamentally about Jesus becoming King of this world and the kingdoms of this world becoming the Kingdom of our God. Therefore, there is no changing of subject matter between the judgments of the Jews and the judgments of Rome. The subject is always the same—it is about expanding the Kingdom. It is about revealing Jesus as King over His enemies: Jews and then Greeks.

Chapter 13
The Return and Marriage

The judgments of God are released in Revelation 4 to 18. Then in Revelation 19, we read about the return of Jesus and the marriage of Jesus to His Bride.

The return of Jesus (commonly referred to as the Second Coming) is the time when Jesus returns to be fully revealed as the triumphant King:

> And on His robe and on His thigh He has a name written, KING OF KINGS, AND LORD OF LORD."
>
> (Rev. 19:16)

When Jesus returns, *"every eye will see Him"* (Rev. 1:7). Then He will rule the nations with a rod of iron (Rev. 19:15).

However, Jesus will not rule alone. Revelation 19 describes the marriage of Jesus to His Bride:

> ...the marriage of the Lamb has come and His bride has made herself ready.
>
> (Rev. 19:7)

It is the Bride and Groom who will reign together.

Full preterists see the return of Jesus and the marriage as having already happened. They happened in A.D. 70 according to full preterists.

Full Preterist View the Return and Marriage at A.D. 70

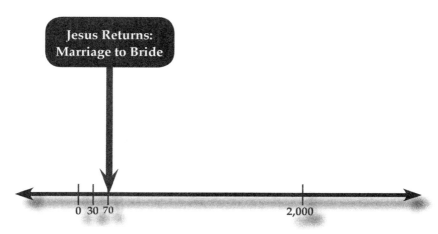

Partial preterists see the return of Jesus and His marriage to the Bride happening in our future. Partial preterists believe in a literal future return, when Jesus will appear in the sky and everyone will see Him.

Partial Preterist View with a Future Return and Marriage

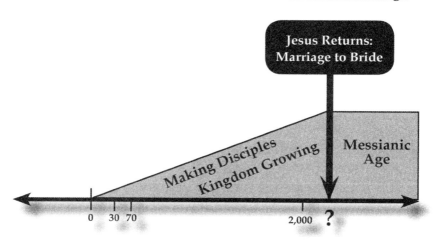

This distinction corresponds with how full preterists and partial preterists read the Book of Revelation. Full preterists see Revelation 19 (which talks about Jesus' return and His marriage) happening simultaneously with the events reported in Revelation 6 to 11, which are happening simultaneously with the events in Revelation 12 to 18. In contrast, partial preterists see the events of Revelation 19 happening after the events of Revelation 1-18.

In reality, there is nothing in the text of the Book that leads the reader to believe the events of Revelation 19 occur simultaneously with the events of Revelation 6-11 or the events of Revelation 12-18. It is only the presuppositions of the full preterists that lead them to read the text as if it repeating the same events over and over.

Chapter 14
The Millennial Reign

Revelation 20 tells us about Jesus reigning for a Millennium.

The word, *millennium*, literally means "1,000 years"; however, the Hebrew people used the number 1,000 to refer to an indefinite number or even forever (*e.g.*, God owns the cattle on 1,000 hills; Ps. 50:10). A millennium can refer to any large, indefinite number.

Because full preterists believe all eschatological prophecies have been fulfilled, they see the millennial reign of Jesus fitting between the enthronement of Jesus at A.D. 30[23] and the destruction of Jerusalem in A.D. 70. As Jesus explained in His parables, the Kingdom grew like seeds in the soil or yeast in dough. According to full preterists, that growth period took place during the 40-year period preceding A.D. 70.

This reveals one of the weakest points of full preterism. The idea that the Millennium only lasted 40 years or less is difficult to swallow. As we stated, a millennium can refer to any large indefinite number, but no where in the Bible or other ancient writings can we find the word *millennium* used to refer to such a small number. Full preterists sometimes deal with this problem by equating the 1,000 years to the "fullness of times," which in their mind could be our Lord completing His judgments by A.D. 70.

To me, this explanation of the full preterists is grasping for straws—straws that do not exists.

---

23 Some full preterists say the Millennium started in A.D. 26 or 27, when Jesus began His public ministry.

Full Preterists' View of the Millennial Reign

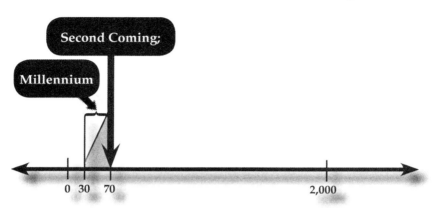

Partial preterists see things differently. They have various views about the Millennium (which I will explain shortly), but they all envision Jesus returning at some point in the future.

As a partial preterist, I believe Jesus will return before the Millennium. This means I hold to the *premillennial view*. This label refers to Jesus returning before (pre) the millennium.

The Millennial Reign During the Messianic Age

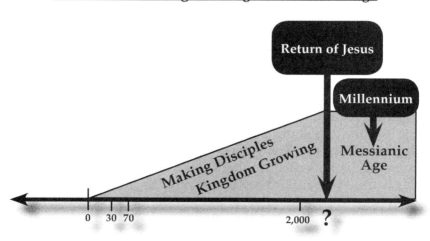

This view is also called *historic premillennialism* because we find it being taught by various leaders throughout Church history. Historic premillennialism is distinguished from dispensational premillennialism, which is the view held by most futurists. The reason their view is called dispensational premillennialism is because of its association with dispensationalism, a theological perspective that divides the Bible, Church history, and the future into distinct time periods.[24]

As I mentioned, many partial preterists see the millennial reign of Jesus differently than I do. Instead of the historic premillennial view, many embrace the *postmillennial view*. These views are similar, except the postmillennialists see the return of Jesus after (post) the millennium. Postmillennialists typically believe the successful preaching of the gospel will usher in a golden age in which Christianity will be the predominate influence on Earth. That golden age will be the Millennium. At the end of that Millennium Jesus will return.[25]

Partial Preterist with a Postmillennial View[26]

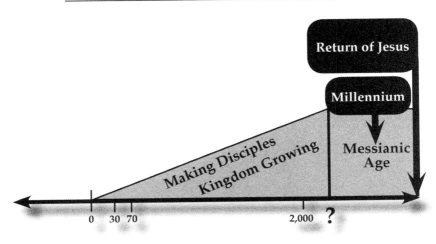

---

24 For a fuller explanation of dispensational premillennialism, consult *Victorious Eschatology*.

25 A small percentage of partial preterists hold to amillennialism.

26 Some postmillennialists see the Millennium starting in A.D. 30.

So then, partial preterists may hold to historic premillennialism or postmillennialism.

I hold to historic premillennialism because I understand the Book of Revelation as reporting consecutive eschatological events. I see the events of chapter 20 (where the Millennium is described) happening after the events of chapter 19 (where Jesus returns and celebrates the marriage feast). In contrast, postmillennialists see the Millennium in chapter 20 overlapping the events of Revelation 4 to 19. I cannot find in the text any break that leads me to believe chapter 20 is a recapitulation of chapters 4 to 19. That seems to me to be a forced interpretation.

Another reason I hold to premillennialism, rather than postmillennialism, is because of my understanding of Satan's activity in the world. That we will discuss in the following chapter.

Chapter 15
Satan Thrown into the Abyss?

Our view of the Millennium determines our understanding of Satan's involvement in the world. Allow me to explain.

Where the Millennium is talked about in Revelation 20, we are told Satan is bound at the beginning of the Millennium:

> *And he laid hold of the dragon, the serpent of old, who is the devil and Satan, and bound him for a thousand years; and he threw him into the abyss, and shut it and sealed it over him, so that he would not deceive the nations any longer...*
>
> (Rev. 20:2-3)

This passage goes on to explain that Satan will be released for a short time at the end of the millennial reign, and then he will be thrown into the Lake of Fire, where he will stay forever (Rev. 20:10).

Since we are told Satan is bound at the beginning of the Millennium, full preterists who are consistent must believe Satan was bound around A.D. 30. Notice that Satan's binding included throwing him into the abyss, shutting it, and sealing it over. Full preterists do see that Satan was released for a short time at the end of the Millennium, but then cast into the Lake of Fire by A.D. 70. According to full preterism, Satan has had no access to this world since A.D. 70.

Full Preterist View of Satan's Activity

As explained in the preceding chapter, I hold to historic premillennialism. This means Satan has not already been removed from the Earth. His removal will happen at the beginning of the Millennium after Jesus returns. He will be released for a short time at the end of the Millennium but then cast into the Lake of Fire.

Partial Preterist View with Historic Premillennialism

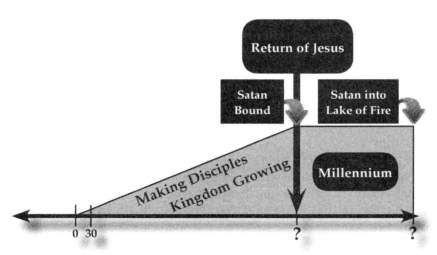

Historic premillennialism does not see Satan as removed from this world yet; however, he no longer has free reign either. When Jesus was enthroned, Satan was dethroned. Paul explained that Jesus *"disarmed the rulers and authorities...He made a public display of them, having triumphed over them"* (Col. 2:15). Jesus said *"the ruler of this world has been judged"* (John 16:11). Satan is no longer god of this world; however, he still is in the world. He is still wandering the Earth seeking someone to devour.

I take the biblical warnings to resist the devil (*e.g.,* James 4:7) as still valid today. Therefore, in order to be consistent, I cannot believe the full preterist view. Satan has not yet been thrown *"into the abyss"* (Rev. 20:3). Therefore, as a partial preterist I hold to historic premillennialism.

Chapter 16
The Great White Throne?

One of the most important distinctions between the partial and full preterist's views has to do with the judgment of all humanity. Revelation 20:11-12 describes the Great White Throne Judgment:

> *Then I saw a great white throne and him who was seated on it...And I saw the dead, great and small, standing before the throne, and books were opened...The dead were judged according to what they had done as recorded in the books.*

Partial preterists believe this passage is describing a future event. There will be a day when all of humanity stands before Jesus, and He will judge them.

Full preterists do not believe in any future judgment of humanity. They teach that the Great White Throne Judgment happened in A.D. 70. Full preterists believe that since A.D. 70 everyone who has died has been immediately judged, then sent to Heaven or hell. There is no future judgment when people will be resurrected from the dead and stand before Jesus. Instead, all people who die are instantly judged and assigned to their eternal dwelling.

At this point, critics of full preterism raise the accusation of being unorthodox. This is because orthodox Christianity has always believed in both the return of Jesus and a future judgment. The Apostles' Creed, which is accepted by the vast majority of Christianity, speaks of Jesus who shall come "to judge the quick and the dead." When this is presented to adherents of full preterism, they will admit their view disagrees with the Apostles' Creed, but they typically respond by saying the Bible is their standard of authority, not the creeds of the Church.

Of course, Christians try to value the Bible as their final and ultimate source for the development of doctrinal truth, but we must not quickly discard such a historic document as the Apostles' Creed. Millions of Christians have studied this creed, and thousands of scholars have concluded that it does express the fundamental doctrines of the Bible.

Furthermore, our forefathers who developed the Nicene Creed (precursor to the Apostles' Creed) in A.D. 325 agreed to the doctrinal statement concerning the return of our Lord to judge the living and dead. This flies in the face of modern full preterism. If the full preterists were correct in their understanding, it seems at least some of our forefathers involved with developing the Nicene Creed would have objected. After all, those forefathers were trying to put down on paper the fundamentals of what the original apostles believed. Those forefathers were closer in time and relationship to the original apostles than we are. They were putting down on paper what the apostles taught so the truths they taught would remain unchallenged in the future.

In spite of this, full preterists hold to their view that there will be no future return or judgment. Therefore, the criticism unorthodox is valid. At the same time, adherents of partial preterism can assure themselves that they do hold to an orthodox eschatological view. In fact, partial preterism was held by the vast majority of our Church fathers whose writings we still have today.

Chapter 17
Resurrection of the Dead

Full preterists do not believe in a future resurrection of the dead. A good way to understand their view is to see how they explain 1 Thessalonians 4:15-17:

> *...we who are alive and remain until the **coming of the Lord**, will not precede those who have fallen asleep. For the Lord Himself will descend from Heaven...and **the dead in Christ will rise first**. Then **we who are alive and remain will be caught up** together with them in the clouds to meet the Lord in the air, and so we shall always be with the Lord.*

In this passage, Paul placed the resurrection at the *"coming of the Lord."* Since full preterists believe there is only one coming (one *parousia*), which they have placed at A.D. 70, they must see the resurrection of the dead as having occurred at A.D. 70.

To see their view more completely, we need to talk separately about *"the dead in Christ who will rise first"* and then how *"we who are alive and remain will be caught up."*

Full preterists believe both groups resurrected in A.D. 70, but the first group consists of all the believers who died before A.D. 70, including the Old Testament saints. Those believers were dead in Hades (*Sheol* in Hebrew), but when Jesus returned in A.D. 70, He transferred them out of Hades into Heaven. As they were transferred, they were given spiritual bodies. That was the time when *"the dead in Christ"* rose. According to full preterists, that was when the resurrection took place.

Full Preterist View of Believers Transferred to Heaven

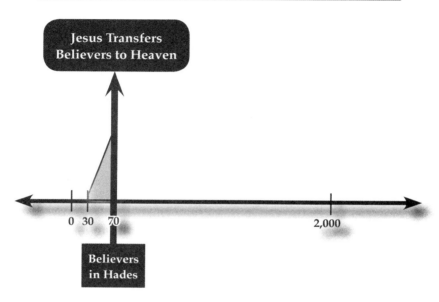

It is true that the Bible talks about Jesus taking dead people from Hades to Heaven. However, the Bible gives us a different timing for that event. It was A.D. 30, not A.D. 70. Peter referred to Jesus descending into Hades during the three days between His death and resurrection (Acts 2:27, 31). Peter also wrote how Jesus:

> ...*died for sins once for all, the just for the unjust, so that He might bring us to God, having been put to death in the flesh, but made alive in the spirit; in which also He went and made proclamation to the spirits now in prison....*
>
> (1 Peter 3:18-19)

Peter went on in that passage to explain how even the people in Noah's day were able to hear the proclamation (3:20), and then

Peter wrote that *"the gospel has for this purpose been preached even to those who are dead"* (1 Peter 4:6). When Jesus ascended out of Hades and into Heaven, He *"led captive a host of captives"* (Eph. 4:8). It was Paul who wrote these words, and since we know he died about A.D. 64, he had to have been writing about an event that had already happened. Matthew even tells us that some of the Old Testament saints who came alive appeared on the streets of Jerusalem (Matt. 27:52-53). That great resurrection took place as Jesus resurrected from the grave in A.D. 30.

Full preterists cannot accept this even though the timing is very clear in Scripture. Full preterists need Jesus' *parousia* and the resurrection to be on the one date in A.D. 70.

Full preterists also have to see A.D. 70 as the date when *"we who are live and remain will be caught up"* (1 Thess. 4:17).

Many full preterists spiritualize this resurrection of those living believers, in the sense of seeing the change that took place in A.D. 70 as a change in God's covenant. Therefore, the living believers were transferred from death into the resurrection life of Jesus. Believers remained on Earth until they died, but they were locked into the new life available through Jesus Christ. They were made to sit with Jesus in heavenly places.

Some full preterists reject the spiritualization of their A.D. 70 resurrection and actually believe a literal rapture of living believers took place in A.D. 70. To support this belief, they will typically point out that we have no writings of Christians for a period of time after A.D. 70. To full preterists, this absence of documentation indicates the believers had been removed from Earth in A.D. 70.[27]

As someone who does not believe in the A.D. 70 rapture, I can point out that we have no historical records of non-Christians writing about the disappearance of Christians. Certainly, the enemies of Christians would have either celebrated or become fearful since they missed the rapture. Furthermore, we know the apostle John was alive well after A.D. 70, so he was not taken up to Heaven in A.D. 70. Obviously, *"we who are alive"* did not get raptured in A.D. 70.

---

27 Some full preterists would say that only the very committed Christians were raptured, while the less committed Christians were left behind.

In contrast to the full preterists' view, partial preterists maintain that there was no rapture in A.D. 70. The transference of believers from Hades to Heaven occurred in A.D. 30 when Jesus resurrected and ascended into Heaven. Partial preterists also believe there will be a future resurrection when:

> ...all who are in the tombs will hear His voice, and will come forth; those who did the good deeds to a resurrection of life, those who committed the evil deeds to a resurrection of judgment.
>
> (John 5:28-29)

Partial Preterist View with a Future Resurrection[28]

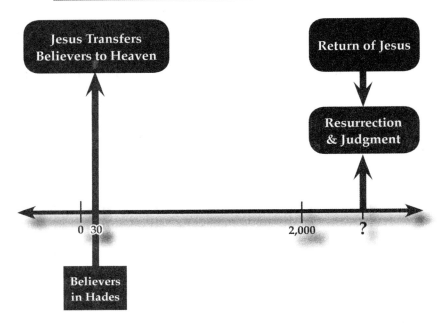

Jesus will return, and the dead will be resurrected to be judged. Again, we can point out that this has always been the view of orthodox Christianity.

---

28 Many teachers identify two resurrections, one at the beginning of the Millennium and another at the end of the Millennium.

Because full preterists do not believe in a future resurrection of the dead, they must explain what happens to people who have died since A.D. 70 and those who will die in our future. Most full preterists explain this by saying that people who die are instantly judged and then go straight to their eternal destiny in Heaven or hell.

This brings up a related issue with which full preterists must deal. They say believers who have died since A.D. 70 are instantly taken to Heaven, but in what form are they taken into Heaven? We know the physical bodies of all people—including Christians—remain here on Earth where they decay and turn into dust. So obviously, Christians do not resurrect in the sense of their physical bodies resurrecting. Full preterists explain this by saying Christians are given spiritual bodies the instant they die and resurrect. Those spiritual bodies are the vessels in which believers spend eternity in Heaven.

This issue of spiritual bodies is a big issue. The reason it is important is because orthodox Christianity has always believed in a future resurrection of the physical bodies of believers. God will take the physical bodies of believers and transform them into incorruptible bodies. This is in contrast to the full preterist view, which says God will not resurrect then transform our physical bodies, but He will give believers completely new spiritual bodies.

Yet, the Bible is clear about the resurrection of our bodies. Paul explained how our physical bodies will be redeemed:

> ...*we ourselves groan within ourselves, waiting eagerly for our adoption as sons, the* **redemption of our body**.
> (Rom. 8:23)

In another passage, Paul explained how:

> *in a moment, in the twinkling of an eye..the dead will be raised imperishable, and we will* **be changed**. *For this perishable must put on the imperishable, and this mortal must put on immortality.*
> (1 Cor. 15:52-53)

Notice that our physical bodies will be changed, not replaced with spiritual bodies. Paul wrote about Jesus:

> Who shall **change our vile body**, that it may be fashioned like unto his glorious body, according to the working whereby he is able even to subdue all things unto himself.
>
> (Phil. 3:21, KJV)

These verses reveal that God is going to use what remains of our physical bodies. Our physical bodies will be resurrected and changed. They will be made immortal.

Some readers may think of this as a minor point. After all, what difference does it make if God makes our new bodies out of our old bodies or if He simply creates brand new bodies for us?

This issue is important for several reasons, one being that Jesus is the first-born of many brethren. When Jesus came out of the grave, His literal body came alive. Consider what happened when Jesus appeared to His disciples after He resurrected:

> But they were startled and frightened and thought that they were seeing a spirit. And He said to them, "Why are you troubled, and why do doubts arise in your hearts? See My hands and My feet, that it is I Myself; touch Me and see, for a spirit does not have flesh and bones as you see that I have."
>
> (Luke 24:37-39)

Jesus showed the disciples that He was not a spirit. He still had hands and feet, flesh and bones. Of course, His body was incorruptible, but He still had a body.

For confirmation that our bodies will be resurrected and transformed, consider Peter's message on Pentecost Day. Peter explained to the multitudes that Jesus rose from the dead. He went on to explain how our Lord's resurrection was foreordained by God. To prove this, Peter quoted the words of King David where David said:

Because You will not abandon my soul to Hades,
Nor allow Your Holy One to undergo decay.

(Acts 2:27)

Peter went on to argue that King David said these words, but not about himself:

Brethren, I may confidently say to you regarding the pa-
triarch David that he both died and was buried, and his
tomb is with us to this day.

(Acts 2:29)

The proof that King David had not resurrected was that his physical body was still in the tomb. Peter understood the resurrection would entail the resurrection of the physical body.

Full preterists cannot accept this truth. Since they believe there will be no future resurrection, they must follow through to the only logical conclusion—that the physical bodies presently laying in the dirt will remain there forever.

A final problem with the full preterists' understanding on the issues related to the resurrection is the location of where resurrected people spend eternity. This issue is best dealt with after we explain the new Heaven and Earth in the chapter that follows.

Chapter 18
New Heaven and Earth

Second Peter 3:3-13 associates the creation of the new Heaven and Earth with the coming (*parousia*) of Christ. Since full preterists believe in only one coming, which happened at A.D. 70, they must assign the creation of the new Heaven and Earth to that one date, A.D. 70.

Full Preterist View with New Earth

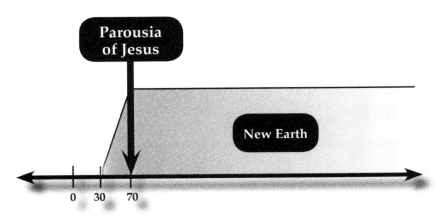

Full preterists equate the new Heaven and Earth with the new covenant. They emphasize 2 Corinthians 5:17, which tells us how *"the old things have passed away; behold, new things have come."* Full preterists claim that all of us Christians live in the new Heaven and Earth right now.

This view can only be developed if a person first embraces the Book of Revelation as fundamentally the testimony of God abolishing the old covenant and establishing the new covenant. As explained in chapter 12, this replacement of covenants is the lens through which full preterists (and some partial preterists) read the Book of Revelation.

In reality, the Book of Revelation is the revelation of Jesus as King. It is the description of the kingdoms of this world becoming the Kingdom of Jesus. This is not to minimize the importance of the new covenant. It is simply to recognize that the covenants are never mentioned in the Book of Revelation. The focus is on King Jesus and His Kingdom.

As noted earlier, the old covenant was made obsolete in A.D. 30, not A.D. 70. Furthermore, the new covenant was 100 percent established in A.D. 30, with the shedding of Jesus' blood. Jesus did it all on the cross, not 40 years later.

If we refrain from seeing the Book of Revelation through the lens of covenant replacement, then we can consider it from the perspective of seeing the Book as a revelation of Jesus Christ as King. First the Jewish enemies were judged, but judgment did not stop there. God the Father told His Son to sit at His right hand until every enemy is put under His feet. Daniel compared the Kingdom to a rock that would grow until it fills the Earth.

If we embrace this understanding of a Kingdom that is growing to the point where every enemy is subjected to King Jesus, then it is logical to think of *the new Earth as that which results from this Kingdom takeover*. With this perspective we see the new Earth beginning, not when Jerusalem was destroyed but when the Kingdom of God has subdued all enemies. Anyone who sees the Book of Revelation through the lens of the growing Kingdom (instead of covenant replacement) will naturally see the new Heaven and Earth existing after every enemy of Jesus has been subdued.

Furthermore, if Christians read the Book of Revelation as a sequence of events, with the events of chapter 21 to 22 occurring after the events of chapter 20, then they will conclude that the new Heaven and Earth will come after the millennial reign. This is true whether Christians hold to historic premillennialism or postmillennialism.

Partial Preterist/Premillennial View with New Earth

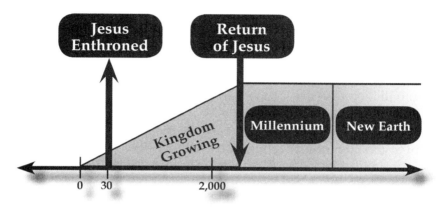

Partial Preterist/Postmillennial View with New Earth

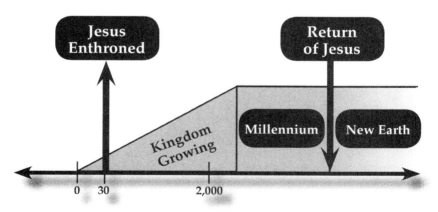

The partial preterist view (premillennial or postmillennial) sees the new Earth going on forever. Jesus will dwell with His people, and they live with Him in a world where there is no sorrow or pain.

Notice how this vision of eternity is different than the view of full preterists. They see people spending eternity in Heaven or hell. Partial preterists envision evil people being cast into hell but believers living eternally on the new Earth.

This distinction can be surprising to many modern Christians because they have been taught that Christians will spend eternity floating in the clouds in Heaven. Yet, that view did not come from the Bible (it came from ancient Greek thought, as we will explain in the chapter to follow). It is okay to refer to our eternal abode as Heaven, but we must keep in mind that Heaven will be on Earth—a new Earth where believers will dwell in glorified physical bodies.

To understand this eternal-earthly-dwelling-place, it is helpful to consider how it comes into existence. Revelation 21:1 says:

> *Then I saw a new Heaven and a new earth; for the first Heaven and the first earth passed away...*

Some Christians take this verse to mean that this present world (Heaven and Earth) will go out of existence, and then God will start fresh, creating an absolutely new world. However, there are some Bible verses that tell us the present Earth is to exist forever. For example, Ecclesiastes 1:4 says:

> *A generation goes and a generation comes,*
> *But the earth remains forever.*

Psalm 78:69 agrees:

> *And He built His sanctuary like the heights,*
> *Like the earth which He has founded forever.*
> (see also, Ps. 104:5)

If we accept these verses that state the eternal nature of the Earth, then we must rethink how this Heaven and Earth can pass away as Revelation 21:1 says.

II Peter 3:5-7 shines some light on this:

> ...the earth was formed out of water and by water, through
> which the world at that time was destroyed, being flooded
> with water. But by His word the present Heavens and
> earth are being reserved for fire, kept for the day of judg-
> ment and destruction of ungodly men.

Notice the comparison Peter is making. He says the present
Heaven and Earth will be destroyed by fire, similarly to how
the Earth was destroyed with water in Noah's day. In Noah's
day, the Earth did not go out of existence, but it was destroyed
in the sense of evil being removed and a new world started.
Similarly, we can think of the present world being judged by
fire, not to go out of existence but to have evil removed and to
go on as a renewed world.

Actually, we should think of the new world as more than
a simple purging of evil, because Revelation 22:3 says that in
the new Heaven and Earth there shall be *"no more curse."* If,
indeed, there will be no more curse, then this includes the removal of the curse resulting from Adam's sin. When that curse
is removed, we should expect that people will no longer have
to work by the sweat of their brow, and there will be no more
dying.

Paul also wrote that creation will be set *"into the freedom of
the glory of the children of God."* This sounds like creation will be
both liberated and responsive to the children of God. No one
can say what this transformation will look like, but it sounds
like it will be a significant change—even glorious!

In summary, we can contrast the vision of eternity held by
partial preterists versus full preterists. Partial preterists see a
future judgment day when evil people will be cast into hell,
while believers will resurrect, have their physical bodies transformed, and then live eternally in the new Heaven and Earth.
In contrast, full preterists envision no future judgment day, but
rather evil people are cast into hell the instant they die, while
believers are resurrected, given spiritual bodies, and then live

in Heaven forever.

Full preterists envision the present Earth going on eternally as it is, with people continuing to reproduce, sinning and repenting, fighting sickness and disease, and working by the sweat of their brow. For full preterists the world is as it always will be. People will live and die, then go to Heaven or hell.

Chapter 19
Redemption of Creation

The discussions of the previous two chapters are vital because they reveal unbiblical conclusions to which full preterism leads. When a system of thought leads to conclusions that are unbiblical then that system of thought is unbiblical. Let me explain.

Full preterism leads one to conclude that the eternal abode for the righteous will be in spiritual bodies floating in an ethereal Heaven for eternity. That way of thinking corresponds with the ancient Greek worldview that saw the natural world as inferior, insignificant, and corrupt. The Greek philosophers saw the human body as a prison in which the soul is confined during its brief stay on Earth. Holding to such a negative view of the natural realm, they envisioned eternal happiness as an age during which people would escape their physical bodies and then move into a higher plane of existence free from the natural, corrupt world.

Throughout the history of the Church many Christians have been influenced by this Greek philosophical worldview. To them it is natural to envision Heaven as a place in the clouds where bodiless people float around doing nothing but smiling and singing. Yet, that way of thinking is foreign to the Bible, which describes people as having glorified yet literal bodies and living on a new Earth where Jesus will come to dwell with

His people forever.

One passage that reveals this distinction between Greek and biblical thought is Acts 17, where Paul was speaking to the philosophers of Athens. Paul ended his dialogue testifying about God's coming judgment, *"having furnished proof to all men by raising Him* [Jesus] *from the dead."* When the Greeks *"heard of the resurrection of the dead, some began to sneer..."* (Acts 17: 31-32). The concept of people being raised from the dead was so contrary to the Greek philosophical worldview that they could not even conceive of it as a possibility.

This difference between Greek and biblical thought was an issue with which the Church battled for many years. Our forefathers believed it so important that they included a confirming statement about the resurrection of the body in the Apostles' Creed:

> *I believe in God the Father, Almighty, Maker of Heaven and earth* [and the]...*resurrection of the body:*

Orthodox Christianity has always held to the belief that people will be resurrected in their physical bodies.

Biblical thought also recognizes the goodness of Earth. It was created as the dwelling place of humanity:

> *The heavens are the heavens of the LORD,*
> *But the earth He has given to the sons of men.*
> (Ps. 115:16)

People were created to have dominion on and over the Earth.

For this reason, it is disturbing to have modern full preterism lead people to conclude that humanity's eternal existence will be in an ethereal spiritual realm.

Of course, this natural world was cursed because of sin, but God's answer is not to destroy it. He is redeeming both creation and humanity. God's solution is to transform this natural world and glorify our physical bodies.

The redemption of the Earth must include the fulfillment of

God's original intentions for humanity to fill Earth and subdue it in the sense of stewarding and caretaking. Humans must someday have dominion over this Earth, in the sense of plants and animals being responsive to people, diseases no longer plaguing humanity, and a world with an abundance for everyone. Isaiah 11:6-9 must be fulfilled: *"the wolf will dwell with the Lamb"* and *"the nursing child will play by the hole of the cobra."* Harmony between nature and humanity must be restored. Creation itself is longing for that day. It longs to be ordered by the gracious stewardship of the children of God. That day will come. Furthermore, *"the earth will be full of the knowledge of the Lord"* (Is. 11:6-9).

Chapter 20
Anti-Semitism?

Full preterists are often accused of being anti-Semitic. In order to address this subject, it is helpful to define the relevant terms. Arranged in the order of positive views toward Jews to the more negative views, those terms are:

1. **Zionism**
2. **One New Man**
3. **Replacement Theology**
4. **Anti-Semitism**

Zionism is the view that believes God has a covenant with the Jews that guarantees them favor above other people on the Earth. Zionists believe the Jews will migrate back to Israel, and when other nations come to destroy them, God will defend the Jews in dramatic ways to the end that Israel will be raised to be one of the mightiest nations on Earth. Christians who hold to this positive view are referred to as Christian Zionists.

At the other extreme is *anti-Semitism,* which refers to a prejudice against and hatred toward the Jews. The most known example of anti-Semitism is from Nazi Germany during World War II. There are certain groups today that cultivate similar anti-Jewish sentiments.

Labeling someone as a Zionist or anti-Semitic is actually determined by one's perspective. Since Zionists believe Jews are favored in God's eyes, anyone who does not believe this may be labeled an anti-Semitic by Zionists. On the other hand, someone who is anti-Semitic may look at Zionists and say they are the ones who are prejudiced by exalting Jews above everyone else.

Less severe than anti-Semitism is *replacement theology*.[29] This is a theological perspective that believes the Jews once were God's chosen people, but the Christian Church has replaced the Jews. According to replacement theology, the natural descendants of Abraham/Israel[30] no longer have special favor in God's eyes any more than any other group of people.

Notice again how one's own perspective determines one's evaluation of someone else's view. For Christian Zionists, replacement theology seems anti-Semitic. Adherents of replacement theology deny they are anti-Semitic but say they see Jews as equal to every other group of people.

One new man is a mediating view between Zionism and replacement theology. Because it is mediating, it is considered moderate in the sense of avoiding extremes. Most people like to think of their own view as avoiding extremes. As a result, many teachers define *one new man* in a way that conforms to their own view. Hence, there is no standard definition that teachers can agree upon, but one aspect of *one new man* that teachers do agree on is the idea that God made a promise to unite Jews and Gentiles under Jesus Christ (Eph. 2:14-16).

Full preterists believe that union happened when Jesus died in A.D. 30. Therefore, we should expect no future fulfillment of this promise for one new man.

In contrast, most Bible teachers who are not full preterists think of one new man as something God will accomplish in the

---

29 Replacement theology is sometimes equated with Supersessionism, which maintains that the natural descendents of Abraham/Israel are no longer considered to be God's chosen people in any sense.

30 The label *descendants of Abraham/Israel* refers to the descendents of Abraham who came through Israel; this is a necessary distinction because not all of Abraham's descendents were included in the Abrahamic covenant; it was the descendents of Israel who received the blessing of Abraham.

future. This view points to Paul's teaching that the Jews were hardened for a time (Rom. 11:7-8), but a day will come in the future when He will open their eyes to recognize Jesus as Messiah. This understanding sees the Jews as still having God's promise that assures them of a future awakening. Therefore, a major revival will take place among the Jews, resulting in Jews and Gentiles worshipping Jesus Christ together.

1. **Zionism:** Jews are God's favored people, with a covenant that assures them of repossession of the Promised Land and an exalted position as a nation.

2. **One New Man:** Jews and Gentiles will be made one under Jesus Christ.

3. **Replacement Theology:** The Church has replaced the Jews as God's favored people.

4. **Anti-Semitism:** The Jews are an inferior race that should be opposed.

Each of these terms is associated with certain eschatological views. For example, futurists are almost always Christian Zionists. They believe the modern Jews should migrate back to Israel, where God will give them the land and favor them over other nations.

Partial preterists are divided over these issues, but I hold to one new man. The natural descendants of Abraham/Israel still have the promise of God that assures them of a future awakening when they will recognize Jesus as Messiah.

Full preterists hold to replacement theology, although most of them will deny this. They typically explain that the natural descendents of Abraham/Israel *never* were God's chosen people. His chosen people have *always* been the people of faith. The Church has always been made up of all people—Jews or Gentiles—who have had faith like Abraham. God's people have always been spiritual Israel, which is the same thing as the Church. According to this way of explaining God's chosen people, the Church did not replace the natural descendents of

Abraham/Israel. The Church did not need to replace the natural descendants because the natural descendents never were God's chosen people.

As I said, people's thoughts on these subjects are determined by their perspective. Since I believe the natural descendents of Abraham/Israel were the recipients of the Abrahamic covenant, the explanation that full preterists offer is, to me, seriously flawed. When full preterists say the natural descendants of Abraham/Israel never were God's chosen people, they are discarding those natural descendents from a position that, to me, is obviously theirs. Although full preterists may deny that they teach replacement theology, their discarding of the natural descendents and claiming that the Church is and has always been spiritual Israel results in the same conclusion as replacement theology. To anyone who does not hold to their view, this is replacement theology.

Still, replacement theology does not necessarily engender any negative attitudes toward the Jews. What does lead to anti-Semitism is the full preterist view that God ended the age of Judaism by pouring out His wrath on them.

It is true that God destroyed Jerusalem and the Temple in A.D. 70. It is also true that God ended the Mosaic covenant in A.D. 30. However, the Bible never equates those events with the end of the age of Judaism. That terminology is never used in the Bible, and I believe it overstates what happened to the Jewish people.

Jesus' description of the judgment of Jerusalem (Matt. 23) reveals that it was against the Jewish religious leaders, not all Jews. Paul argued that God did not reject all of the Jews, but He kept a remnant for Himself even through their periods of disobedience (Rom. 11:1-5). This is evidenced by the fact that most of the early Christians were Jews. Acts 6:7 even tells us that a *"great many of the priests were becoming obedient to the faith."* Jesus explained that every Jewish scribe:

> who has become a disciple of the kingdom of heaven is
> like a head of a household, who brings out of his treasure

things new and old.

(Matt. 13:52)

What the Jewish people had before Jesus came was not evil. Jesus saw it as treasures which produce great blessings when combined with the treasures of the Kingdom.

Paul talks about some Jews being broken off and then Christians being grafted into the *"rich root of the olive tree"* (Rom. 11:17-24). The imagery used here implies the continuation of the people who inherited the blessings of the Abrahamic covenant. God did not end the age of Judaism, but rather He removed some of the natural descendents of Abraham, while grafting in believing Gentiles.

Rather than say it was the end of the age of Judaism, it is more accurate to say that it was the beginning of the age when God reached out to all of humanity. God is now offering the blessings of Abraham and a better covenant to all who put their faith in Jesus.

In Closing

As a traveling minister, I speak at churches and conferences hosted by many different denominations with various doctrinal persuasions. Several of my friends oversee ministries that hold to the full preterist view. They know I disagree with them, but our friendship and common grounds in Jesus Christ far outweigh our differences.

In the process of ministering together, the implications of our different eschatological views occasionally come to the forefront. It is unnecessary to explain any more of those doctrinal differences, but it may be helpful to briefly mention some of the practical outworking of their eschatology. Hence, you can know what to expect from full preterist groups with whom you come in contact.

For example, you may be surprised to learn that most full preterists consider the Lord's Prayer as non-applicable to modern Christianity. They see the phrase, "Your Kingdom come, Your will be done," as already fulfilled, and therefore, saying this prayer any time after A.D. 70 is misguided.

Their understanding of the Kingdom and the Millennium determines their view of Satan's activity in this world. Full preterists believe Satan has already been removed from the Earth. Most full preterists extend this understanding to all demons, so they have no reason to fight or resist demons. According to them, the only war we have today is with our own carnality and the evil of humanity around us.

Some (let me emphasize, not all) full preterists see the Great Commission as not applicable for us today. Jesus said to His disciples:

> *Go therefore and make disciples of all the nations, baptiz-*
> *ing them in the name of the Father and the Son and the*
> *Holy Spirit...and lo, I am with you always, even to the*
> *end of the age.*
>
> (Matt. 28:19-20)

Full preterists point out our Lord's reassuring words that He would be with them *"even to the end of the age."* Since they believe the end of the age came in A.D. 70, some full preterists see the Great Commission as only directed toward those who lived before A.D. 70.

Notice also in the Great Commission how Jesus instructed His disciples to water baptize believers. Some full preterist groups see these instructions as only applying to the early Christians up until the time of Jesus' *parousia* in A.D. 70.

Not only is the ordinance of water baptism questioned, but so also is the Lord's Supper. Full preterists point to Paul's words of instruction:

> *For as often as you eat this bread and drink the cup, you*
> *proclaim the Lord's death until He comes.*
>
> (1 Cor. 11:26)

According to these words, the purpose of the Lord's Supper was to proclaim the Lord's death *"until He comes."* Since full preterists believe Jesus came in A.D. 70, they conclude the Lord's Supper should no longer be practiced.

The decision to not practice communion or water baptism is also due to their general emphasis on the Jewish religious practices being abolished. The underlying idea of God not desiring His people to practice religious rituals or ordinances of any kind is strong within full preterist groups.

A smaller number of full preterists are sceptical of any leadership positions in the Church. They quote Ephesians 4:11-12, which tells us of Jesus giving apostles, prophets, evangelists, pastors, and teachers for the equipping of the saints:

until we all attain to the unity of the faith, and of the knowledge of the Son of God, to a mature man, to the measure of the stature which belongs to the fullness of Christ.

(Eph. 4:13)

Since full preterists believe God has fulfilled everything that is written, many believe the Church has already attained to the unity of the faith and full maturity. Being consistent with this idea, some full preterists see no need for leaders in the Church.

This way of thinking is reinforced when full preterists explain their view that all of the provisions of the new covenant have been fulfilled, including Jeremiah's words:

They will not teach again, each man his neighbor and each man his brother, saying, "Know the Lord," for they will all know Me, from the least of them to the greatest of them...

(Jer. 31:34)

If, indeed, this promise has been fulfilled, then we do not need teachers in the Church any longer.

Finally, we can point out how most full preterists have no place for the charismatic gifts in the modern Church. First Corinthians 13:10 talks about gifts of tongues and prophecy being around until *"the perfect comes."* Since full preterists believe the perfect has come, it is natural for them to conclude that the spiritual gifts have passed away. This includes miracles, which most full preterists see as God's supernatural empowering to get the early Christians through the intense period of persecution preceding the A.D. 70 destruction.

Not all full preterist share the beliefs mentioned above, but they are fairly common. If a group does embrace any of the practices mentioned above, such as water baptism or charismatic gifts, then they will offer alternative explanations as to why they continue.

In spite of these non-traditional beliefs, I find full preterists to be very devout Christians, knowledgable of the Bible, and sincere in their walk with God. Even though we disagree, they are our brothers and sisters in Christ.

Other Books by Harold R. Eberle

Christianity Unshackled

Most Christians in the Western world have no idea how profoundly their beliefs have been influenced by their culture. What would Christianity be like if it was separated from Western thought? After untangling the Western traditions of the last 2,000 years of Church history, Harold R. Eberle offers a Christian worldview that is clear, concise, and liberating. This will shake you to the core and then leave you standing on a firm foundation!

Compassionate Capitalism:
A Judeo-Christian Value

As you read this book, you will learn how capitalism first developed as God worked among the Hebrew people in the Old Testament. The resulting economic principles then transformed Western society as they spread with Christianity. However, our present form of capitalism is different than that which God instilled in Hebrew society. What we need to do now is govern capitalism wisely and apply the principles of capitalism with compassion.

Releasing Kings for Ministry in the Marketplace

By John S. Garfield and Harold R. Eberle

"Kings" is what we call Christian leaders who have embraced the call of God upon their lives to work in the marketplace and from that position transform society. This book explains how marketplace ministry will operate in concert with local churches and pastors. It provides a Scriptural basis for the expansion of the Kingdom of God into all areas of society.

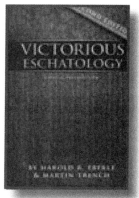

Victorious Eschatology
Coauthored by
Harold R. Eberle and Martin Trench

Here it is—a biblically-based, optimistic view of the future. Along with a historical perspective, this book offers a clear understanding of Matthew 24, the book of Revelation, and other key passages about the events to precede the return of Jesus Christ. Satan is not going to take over this world. Jesus Christ is Lord and He will reign until every enemy is put under His feet!

Jesus Came Out of the Tomb... So Can You!
A Brief Explanation of
Resurrection-based Christianity

Forgiveness of sins is at the cross. Power over sin is in the resurrection and ascension. Yet, most Christians have no idea how to access the benefits of our Lord's resurrection and ascension. They are locked into death-centered Christianity, rather than life-centered Christianity. This book empowers the reader to make the transition and "come out of the tomb."

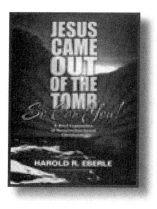

Grace...the Power to Reign
The Light Shining from Romans 5-8

We struggle against sin and yearn for God's highest. Yet, on a bad day it is as if we are fighting against gravity. Questions go unanswered:

•Where is the power to overcome temptations?

•Is God really willing and able to breathe into us so that our dry bones can live and we can stand strong?

For anyone who has ever struggled to live godly, here are the answers.

Precious in His Sight
(Third edition)
A Fresh Look at the Nature of Humanity

How evil are we? How can I love myself if I am evil? What happened when Adam sinned? How does that sin influence us? Where do babies go when they die? This book has implication upon our understanding of sin, salvation, who God is, evangelism, and how we live the victorious Christian life.

Who Is God?

Challenging the traditional Western view of God, Harold R. Eberle presents God as a Covenant-maker, Lover, and Father. Depending on Scripture, God is shown to be in a vulnerable, open and cooperative relationship with His people. This book is both unsettling and enlightening—revolutionary to readers—considered by many to be Harold's most important contribution to the Body of Christ.

Developing a Prosperous Soul
Vol. I: How to Overcome a Poverty Mind-set
Vol. II: How to Move into God's Financial Blessings

There are fundamental changes you can make in the way you think which will help you release God's blessings. This is a balanced look at the promises of God with practical steps you can take to move into financial freedom. It is time for Christians to recapture the financial arena. These two volumes will inspire and create faith in you to fulfill God's purpose for your life.

Other Books by Harold R. Eberle

God's Leaders for Tomorrow's World
(Revised/expanded edition)

You sense the call to leadership, but questions persist: "Does God want me to rise up? Do I truly know where to lead? Is this pride? How can I influence people?" Through an understanding of leadership dynamics, learn how to develop godly charisma. Confusion will melt into order when you see the God-ordained lines of authority. Fear of leadership will change to confidence as you learn to handle power struggles. It is time to move into your "metron," that is, your God-given sphere of authority.

The Complete Wineskin
(Fourth edition)

The Body of Christ is in a reformation. God is pouring out His Holy Spirit and our wineskins must be changed to handle the new wine. Will the Church come together in unity? How does the anointing of God work and what is your role? What is the 5-fold ministry? How are apostles, prophets, evangelists, pastors, and teachers going to rise up and work together? Where do small group meetings fit in? This book puts into words what you have been sensing in your spirit. (Eberle's best seller, translated into many languages, distributed worldwide.)

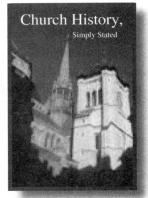

Church History,
Simply Stated

How did the Church get to where She is today? How did we get so many denominations? Who are the leaders who formed our thoughts? Where is the Church going? To fully answer these questions requires a knowledge of the past. Here is a simple, concise explanation of Church history. With two or three hours of reading, anyone can develop a clear picture of our Christian heritage.

The Spiritual, Mystical, and Supernatural

The first five volumes of Harold R. Eberle's series of books entitled, Spiritual Realities, have been condensed into this one volume, 372 pages in length. Topics are addressed such as how the spiritual and natural worlds are related, angelic and demonic manifestations, signs and wonders, miracles and healing, the anointing, good versus evil spiritual practices, how people are created by God to access the spiritual realm, how the spirits of people interact, how people sense things in the spirit realm, and much more.

To place an order or to check current book prices:

Web Site: www.worldcastpublishing.com
E-mail: office@worldcastpublishing.com

509-248-5837

Worldcast Publishing, P.O. Box 10653
Yakima, WA 98909-1653

On-line Bible College:
Institute for Hope and Life

- Study at home
- Earn a certificate, Associates degree or
     Bachelors degree
- Study and proceed at your own rate

- Several courses taught by Harold R. Eberle
- Many other outstanding instructors from
     Vision International Education Network.

http://instituteforhopeandlife.com